CRUISER MANAGEMENT

Colin Jones

Helmsman Books

First published in 1992 by
Helmsman Books, an imprint of
The Crowood Press Ltd
Ramsbury, Marlborough
Wiltshire SN8 2HR

British Library Cataloguing in Publication Data

A catalogue record for this book is available from the British Library

ISBN 1 85223 700 7

Picture credits

Photographs by Colin Jones.
Line-drawings by Jan Sparrow.

Typeset by Avonset, Midsomer Norton, Avon
Printed in Great Britain by Redwood Press Ltd, Melksham, Wilts.

CONTENTS

	Introduction	5
1	Turning on the Power	8
2	The Cruiser Managers	23
3	Let's Go to Sea	33
4	Anchoring – The Forgotten Art	41
5	Berthing	60
6	Unberthing	82
7	The Amateur Professional	88
8	Get the Right Equipment	96
9	Across the Channel	112
	Glossary	125
	Index	127

INTRODUCTION

In the cruiser's vocabulary, Pride is not one of the Seven Deadly Sins. With us, it is an essential virtue. If you have a personal pride in the things that you do at sea, they will probably be done well. That makes you much safer and gives you considerably more satisfaction and fun.

These sentiments are echoed in a segment pencilled into my own cruising notebook diary, written some hundred nautical miles out into the notorious Bay of Biscay.

'Yesterday, I awoke to cold summer rain and wind with the boat heaving and rolling like a seven-ton bull. I asked myself what I was doing out here and swore to sell the whole outfit just as soon as I could get it back to the land. Then I noticed just how

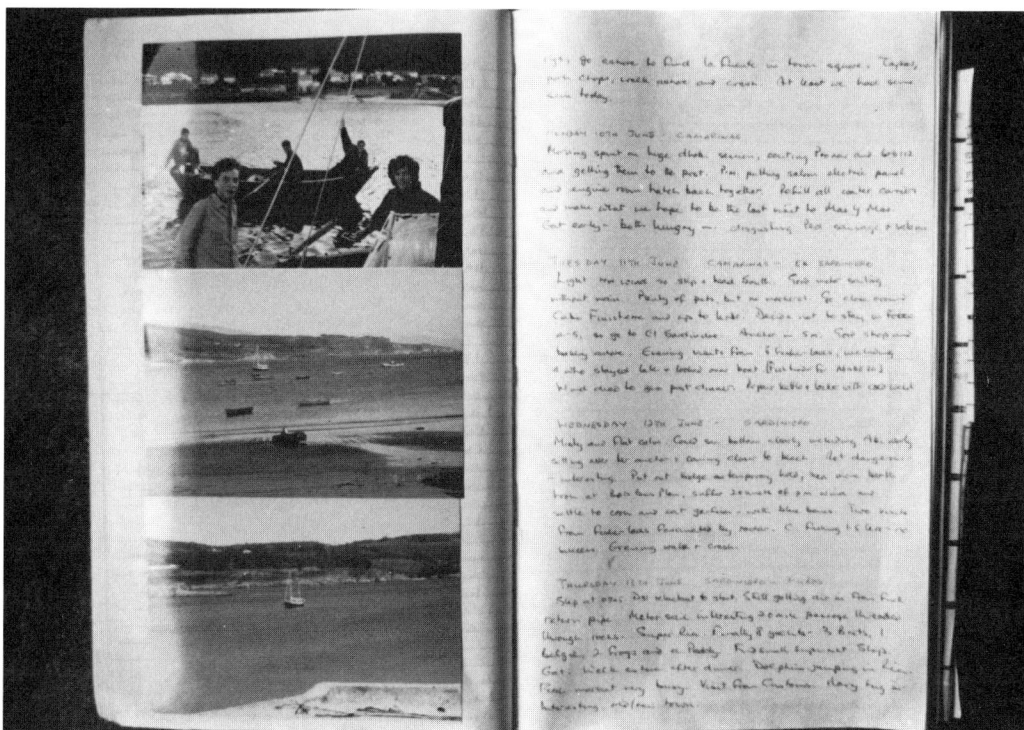

A cruiser notebook is worth keeping.

well the sails were balanced and the way that all the navigation systems were purring and working well and my sourness turned to pride.

'It felt even better this morning, when I took my coffee onto the warm, sun-blessed foredeck and looked back along the length of our well found little ship, now two hundred miles across the Bay, spanking along with all three sails pulling hard and steady to a wind on the quarter. I reflected over the years that we have owned *Abemama* and just how much time and effort have been put into making her that way. Immediately I forgave and forgot that the need to keep watches at night had left me short of sleep and that the boat swallows up absolutely every penny of our spare cash.

'Before my pride puffed too high, I noticed that even though it was now full daylight, the steaming lights were still on. It did not really matter because there was not another vessel within twenty miles at least, but your pride in your seamanship – in doing things properly – makes you abandon the coffee and hurry aft to switch them off.'

'Doing things properly' has to be the cruising crew's leitmotiv. Your social lives and even your actual lives depend on how meticulously you prepare your boat and on how efficiently you manage all her departments, whether she is fitting out ashore, or bowling down to Biscay with a north-easter on her tail.

Cruising is a bug, and financing, handling and generally managing boats well is part of the passion. Sit for a while in any marina and you are sure to join the amusement and mocking that is directed towards anyone who handles a boat very badly. This mismanagement occasionally happens because the yacht is short of some

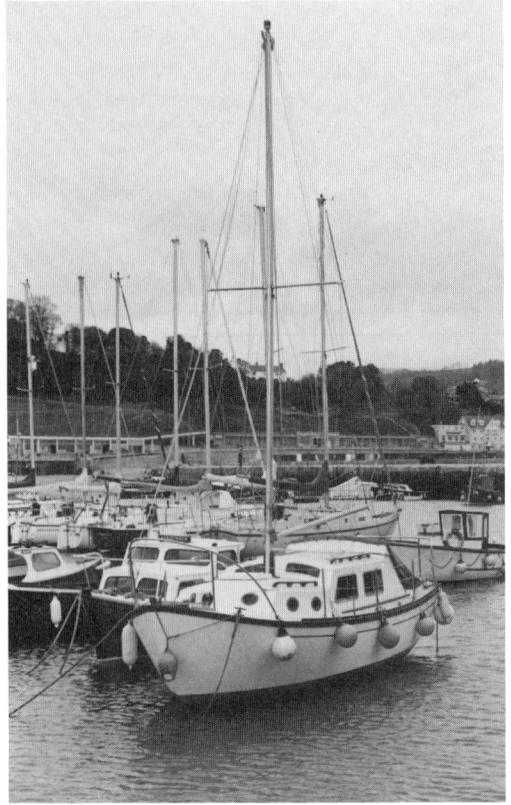

Even a snug motor sailer cruises well.

essential equipment, or the skipper himself is lacking in knowledge of how to use it.

Equally, my cruising partner and I sat in Cherbourg and admired an elderly couple who had mistakenly taken a 15m (49ft) ketch into a line of berths where there was not a free space. The woman stood at the bow with a glass of something in one hand, whilst she used the other to relay a series of signals to the man on the tiller and gear shift. With absolutely no word spoken between them, they turned the boat round short, in a space that was only about 3m (10ft) longer than their hull, then went back down the space between the pontoons to find a free berth elsewhere. The manoeuvre was so well done that it earned a spontaneous round of applause from the dozen lounging crews who were watching.

We later visited the couple on board and were not really surprised to find a crew confident in their ability to deal with any situation and a vessel well enough equipped to be everything from a floating workshop to a palace of entertainment. She was a very well-managed, total, little ship.

That duo will never be afraid to take any boat anywhere, no matter what its size. Big? Small? It does not really matter. Properly set up 6m (19ft) cruisers regularly cross the Atlantic with ease. Those who fit them out and who handle them so well will make the transition to a bigger boat with absolutely no difficulty. Some of the best boat management is learned by children with their first dinghies.

However, by far the greatest number of cruising boats fall into the 6–12m (20–40ft) bracket. The range represents a dream and a reality and it is where most of the material in these pages is aimed at. Even if the dream is not immediately attainable for many of us, it can be affordable for anyone who wants a boat badly enough to take on the buying and learning commitment that cruising connotes.

It is hoped that the advice and educational anecdotes in these pages will help the newcomer to cruising to do it without apprehension. I suspect that even the experienced will get a little something from it, in exactly the same way that I myself never stop learning and am constantly gleaning new ideas from material penned by my colleagues in the 'academy' of marine authors.

Good and safe sailing to you.
Start it right here.

1

TURNING ON THE POWER

In talking of cruising boats, the phrase 'turning on the power' connotes a more complex topic than such a simple boat task ought to. Power is the force that causes a boat to move. In its simplest form, boat inertia is overcome by the sails and/or the engine. But a boat can also be moved by the wind, even when no sails are set. It can also be bodily shifted by river currents, tide and the effects created by other vessels. These same forces will arrest progress through the water in a number of directions.

No matter what the motive power, a hull can, will and does move forwards, backwards and sideways, or will be displaced as the product of any of these forces, which simply means that the boat's mass will move on a diagonal. It may do this of its own volition, or it can be deliberately set to go in any of these directions, or even to pivot about its own axis.

You should already be beginning to get a picture of just how omni-directional the movements of a marine vehicle can be. A good skipper is constantly making observations and judgements and only rarely will he think that his boat is travelling in a dead straight line. Knowing this means that he can always be using these interacting components of force to his best advantage. Even in the calm of a marina,

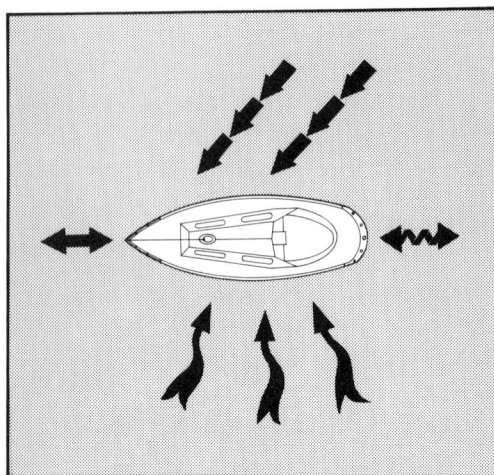

Many forces can move or stop a boat.

the good boat handler is using the boat's unavoidable ability to go sideways as much as he is harnessing its main thrusts ahead and astern.

In addition to causing boats to move, the elements of force mentioned above also cause boats to stop. We have no brakes, so we stop the boat by applying propeller thrust in the opposite direction, or by turning her into the wind or the current, to let their counter forces bring her to a halt. Unfortunately, this usually produces its own quirky directional effects, which we shall discuss as we go along.

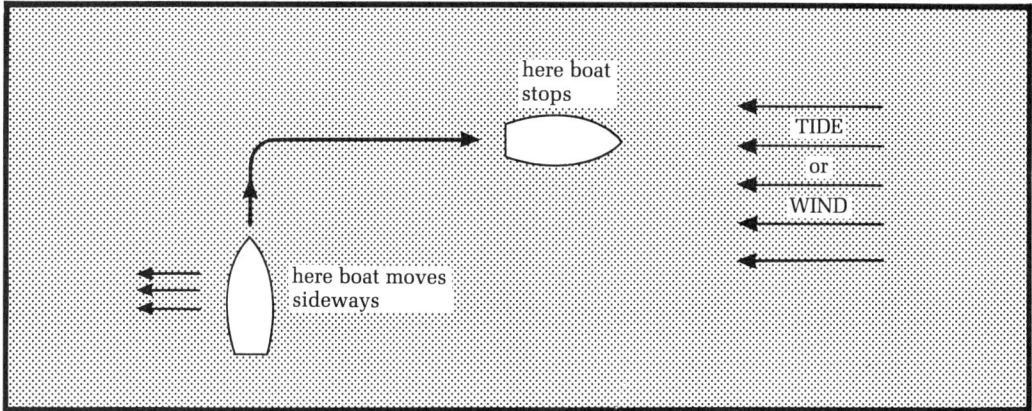

Turning into wind or tide is like putting the engine astern to stop the boat.

Had I been writing this book twenty years ago, I could not have done other than include separate chapters for sailing craft and motor boats. However, social and practical demands, married to engineering progress, have moved us all towards the centre. Modern diesel engines give such enormous power from small, lightweight units that the trend is to give even quite small yachts very powerful motors.

This makes sense in our crowded harbours and marinas, where an underpowered boat can cause considerable damage to herself and to others. We are also constrained by our more hectic lives and an inadequate supply of parking places. Many skippers are anxious to find a good pontoon or harbour wall berth for the night, before all the best spaces are taken up by less deserving early arrivals so, rather than beat to windward, they fire up the diesel and make haste.

Additionally, these small engines offer an easier facility to fit twin-power units to cruising, sailing craft – and this is increasingly happening. In many senses, most of us who go cruising are motor sailers these days.

The complete cruising skipper, everywhere from the blue waters far off-shore, through the fickle winds along the cliffs, right up until he picks up a buoy or puts his fenders alongside a fixed berth, will be using all of the power sources at his disposition.

The Single-screw Cruiser

It is surprising how few boat owners know the characteristics of their propellers and the effects that a twisting paddle has on the hull's linear progress. A boat prop is specified in terms of diameter, pitch and whether it is 'left hand' or 'right hand'. It is usual to refer all propeller data to the view from astern of the boat. From here a right-hand prop rotates clockwise and vice versa.

Prop Walking

This is common to all boats. The action of a propeller blade in the top quarter of its rotation has much the same action as a paddle. As it swings through its first 90

A right-handed prop.

degrees it literally pulls the stern of the boat sideways – just like a claw.

All boats suffer from this phenomenon, which is scarcely noticed in normal forward drive. It also means, however, that they all turn tighter and more readily one way than to the other. A vessel with a right-hand prop will generally turn best to port because the stern is being clawed out to starboard.

This action can be either an embarrassment, or of use when coming alongside, when you will generally need a burst of reverse prop. The good skipper will use it with confidence when getting into small spaces and will even select his direction of approach for best prop use. My own boat, for example, has a left-hand prop that

Walking action of the prop.

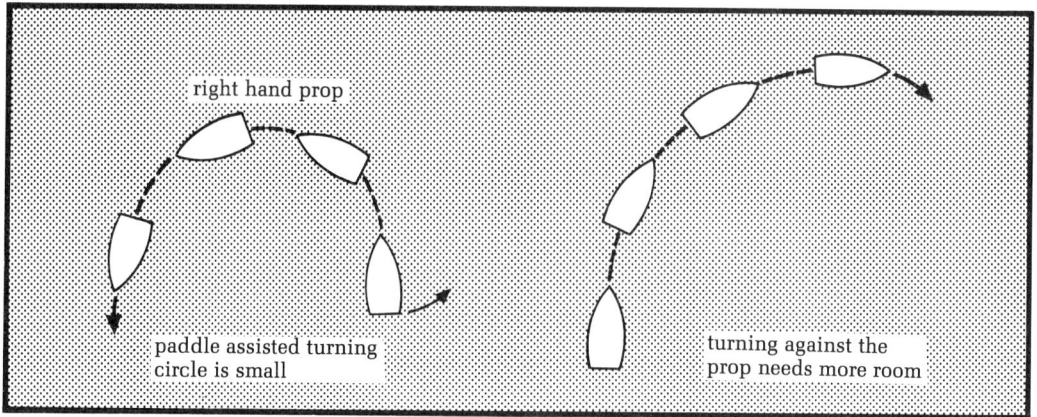

Comparison of turning with the prop or against it.

causes the stern to kick very hard to starboard when put astern. If I am turning right to get into a pontoon slot, I can swing the boat fast and hard to starboard, knowing that the turn will stop immediately I reverse the engine. Equally, I can use this starboard thrust to kick the stern into the quay if I am berthing 'starboard side to'.

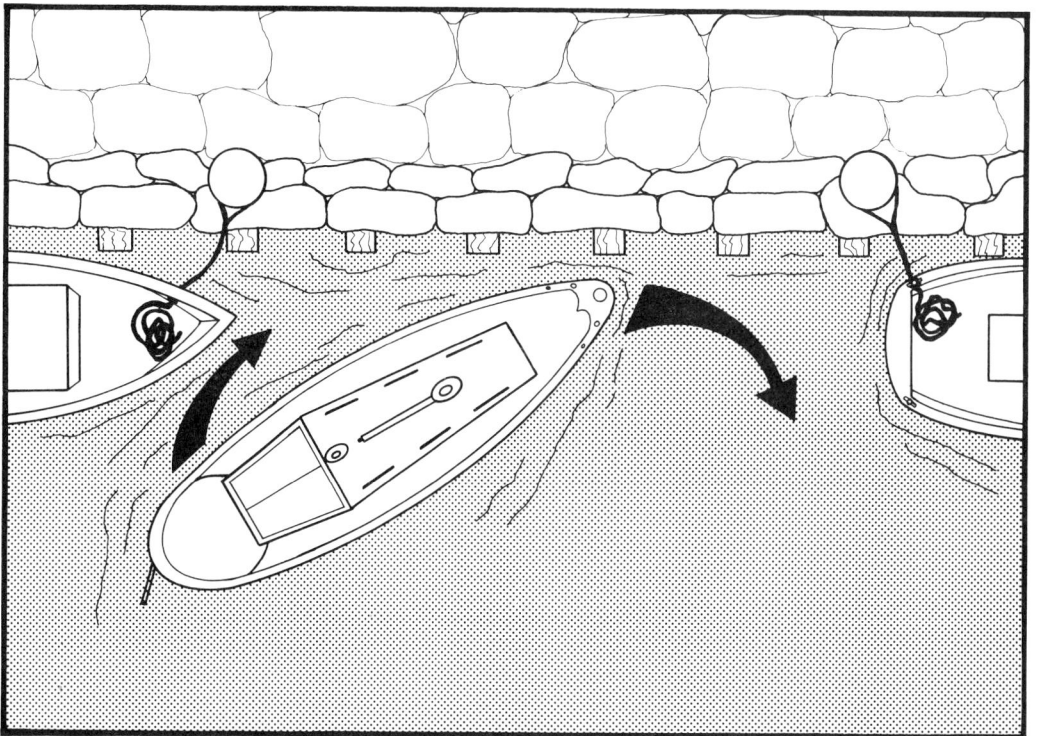

Port side to in a small space.

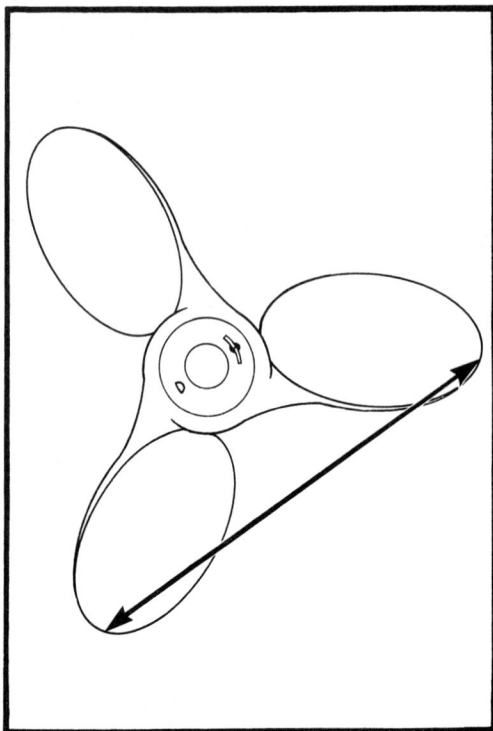

Prop diameter is measured across the circumference.

Propeller Diameter

This is simply the measurement across the blades at their very tip. Put another way, it is the diameter of the circle prescribed by the rotating unit. The larger the prop, the greater the swept area of its blades and the more thrust it creates per revolution. Generally speaking, a smaller propeller will give better acceleration, whilst a large prop means lower engines revs, a greater linear distance per spin and better cruising fuel economy – as long as boat and engine can cope with the load.

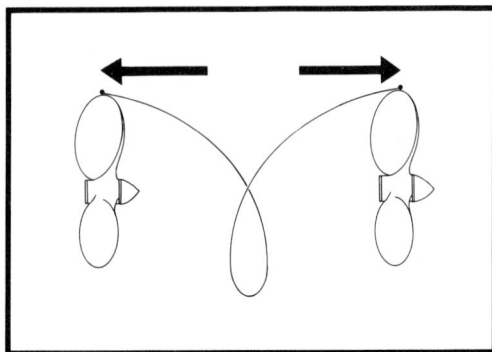

Screwing action defines propeller pitch.

Propeller Pitch

This cannot be divorced from diameter. They always go together. Pitch is the distance that the propeller would 'screw' itself through completely still water in one revolution, with no allowance being made for slippage. If this distance is small, the prop is said to be of fine pitch. A coarse-pitch propeller obviously demands more engine power: it will give slower hull acceleration and can have a very pronounced effect on engine performance, because it makes the boat move further per revolution. It has more work to do per spin.

Propeller Balance

Balancing the diameter and the pitch against each other is a job for a technical expert who, these days, generally employs a computer-calculated formula, which is the product of overall length, beam, weight and engine size. He will then quote a two-figure specification of diameter and pitch, in that order.

As a rough guide, a well-balanced prop will let the engine rev to about 75 per cent of the range it would reach in neutral (unloaded), and will permit the boat to achieve something close to its hull speed.

Our own 9m (30ft), 7.5-tonne (7.4-ton) motor sailer is driven by a 37,285-watt (50-hp)/2.2-litre (4 pint) BMC diesel. When we took her over, we were disappointed with her speed under engine and by the fact that the prop seemed to have no real 'grip' on the water – it did not kick out a good backwash. Even more worrying was the observation that we could get 3,200 rpm in neutral and almost the same in gear. To get a moderate cruising speed of 5 knots, we were doing 2,600 rpm and were falling 2 knots short of hull speed at maximum revs in forward gear.

Out of the water, we discovered that the fitted prop was a $17 \times 11 \times 3$ blader. There is plenty of room in the hull's propeller aperture, leaving a good space between the top of the arc and the bottom of the boat. A consultation suggested that 18×12 was ideal, so we fitted the $17\frac{1}{2} \times 12\frac{1}{2}$ spare as a very near compromise.

The boat now does an easy 5 knots at 1,800 rpm and is up to $7-7.5$ knots (which is very close to maximum for the hull) at full revs. In gear, we can achieve 2,900 rpm, but cruising at just below 2,000 rpm we still burn only $2-3$ litres (0.5 gallons) of diesel per hour, reducing to 1.5 litres (0.33 gallons) when we are motor sailing at 1,200 rpm minus, which might give anything from 4.5 knots to 7.0 knots, depending on the external circumstances.

The instance is quoted to show just how important propeller balance can be. If you get it wrong, your boating becomes more expensive not only in the day-to-day sense, but also in the strain that is put on the engine and in general misuse of the diesel injectors.

The ideal solution to most propeller problems would be the superefficiency of

The larger prop works very well.

a single-bladed thrust unit with infinitely variable pitch. Unfortunately, a single blader would create enormous vibration, and variable pitch props are expensive. Thus, most of us are offered two-bladed auto-fold props for pure sailing racers that require only a small auxiliary power unit, or we fit smooth-turning three bladers for boats that require the engine to do rather more work.

The reduction gearbox also tends to be a bit misunderstood. Its basic function of reducing engine revs to a level more acceptable by the propeller and shaft (e.g. 2:1) is not a mystery, whilst the fore and aft shift gearing can be seen from any manufacturer's diagram. Most beginner

The all-important stern gland grease point.

boaters have problems understanding the lubrication system and the shaft connection.

It is essential to check on how your gearbox and shaft are lubricated. Our own is not untypical: the gearbox itself is lubricated (and its lube oil is cooled) by the engine. This means that it is unlubricated and at risk if we go for very long periods in pure sailing mode with the shaft turning. Some sort of shaft brake is essential if you sail long distances, or if the boat is moored in a river whose current is strong enough to turn the prop. Some skippers lock the shaft with mole grips, but a proper shaft brake operated by a pressure switch is a much safer idea.

Most prop shafts are kept lubricated and cooled by sea water sucked into the bearing and the stuffing box via two small holes in the outer housing. If the shaft runs hot, it may well be that these are clogged. If the stuffing box/gland lets in sea water, this is more inconvenient than dangerous, and indicates that the unit is short of grease.

We recently met a skipper complaining that his stern gland leaked so much that thirty minutes' pumping was needed every four to five days, even though he tightened up the grease gland 'two or three times every season'. Our own gland has a 15cm (6in) grease reservoir tube and is tightened every six hours on a long run.

Before we leave the boat on the moorings, the stern gland grease pressure is one of the last things we check. It gets turned down until no drips are coming in.

The Twin-screw Cruiser

A boat with dual contra-rotating props is probably everybody's ideal boat when it comes to handling in confined spaces. (The safety of twin engines on long hauls is also the stuff of dreams.) The props are set to rotate in opposite directions to counteract the 'walking' effect described earlier, which would be exaggerated by their off-centre installation. The usual method is to have them both turning

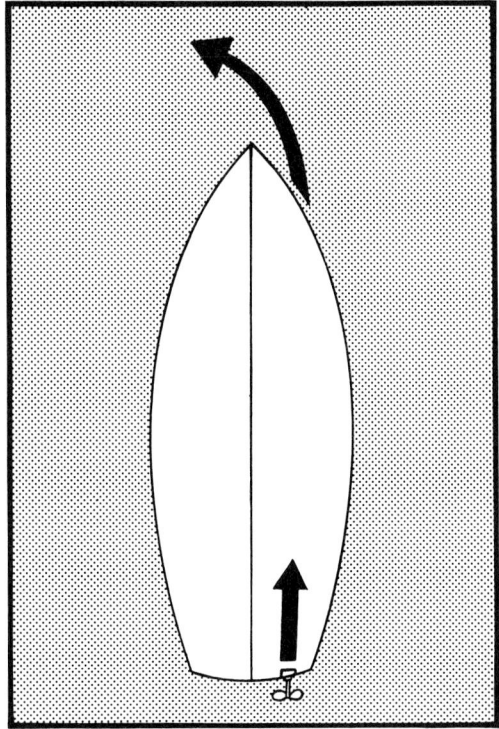

Single-screw turning.

Contra-rotating props for maximum efficiency.

outward when engaged ahead – left-hand prop to port and right-hand going clockwise.

The way to visualize their turning action when engaged separately is to think of the chosen prop as pushing (or pulling) its own side of the boat, whilst the other side remains stationary. The starboard prop, going ahead, tends to push the hull in a circle prescribed around the stationary port side and vice versa. Putting the port engine astern pulls the port side in a backwards circle around its opposite. This is the beauty of twin screws. With one pushing ahead and the other pulling astern, the boat can be turned almost in its own length.

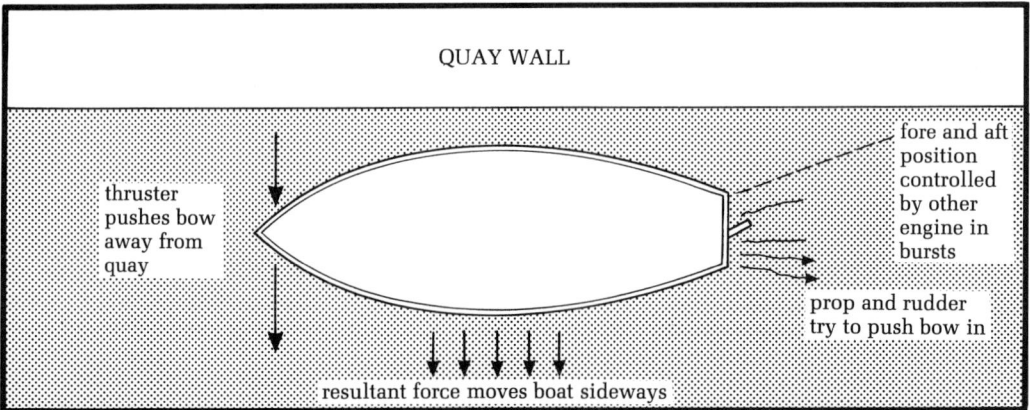

Walking the boat sideways with prop and bow thruster.

A **bow thruster** used in tandem with twin screws is even better. Modern bow props are, for the most part, electrically driven units housed in a thwartship hole in the keel, or they are mounted on a hydraulic arm that retracts vertically into the hull when not in use.

A proficient skipper, using twin screws and a bow thruster, will be able to make the boat walk sideways out of a tight berth. Imagine him port side to the quay, with the bow thruster set to push the front of the boat away and the starboard engine set ahead. By playing the engine and thruster revs against each other a tension is created to push to starboard. Gentle use of the 'spare' port motor will maintain the boat's fore and aft place in the gap and out she comes.

Rudder Effects

The rudder turns the boat by being angled to the direction of the backwash created by the propeller. If this current is deflected to starboard, it pushes the stern of the boat to port in a practical expression of the Law of

Motion that decrees that action and re-action are equal and opposite. The turning movement is created by a flow of water over the rudder blade, with a more vigorous reverse jet causing a sharper turn than a weaker current. This is why the boat steers more positively when the prop is turning than when water flow is due only to passage through that medium. When the boat is stopped, the rudder does not turn the hull at all.

From this it will be seen that when the rudder is offset at an angle of fifteen to thirty degrees, it will turn the boat quite effectively. When it gets out at right angles to the line of the prop wash and the keel, it ceases to apply any turn and merely acts as a very inefficient brake.

Propeller Maintenance

Some final advice on propellers would be not to neglect regular inspection, even if your boat is a fin keeler with a prop well down in the water.

Propellers work best when they are clean, bright and free of weed and have no

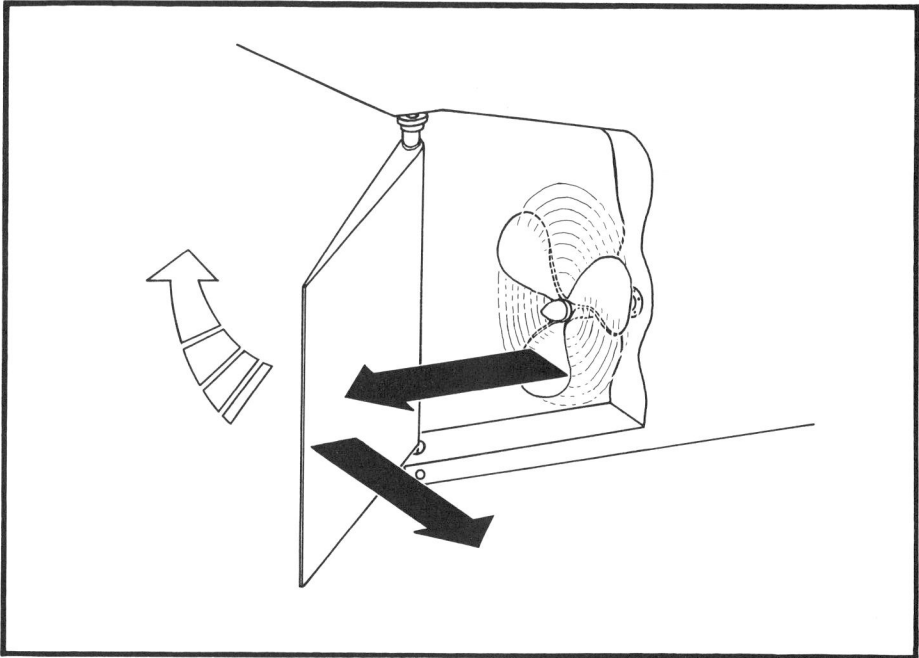

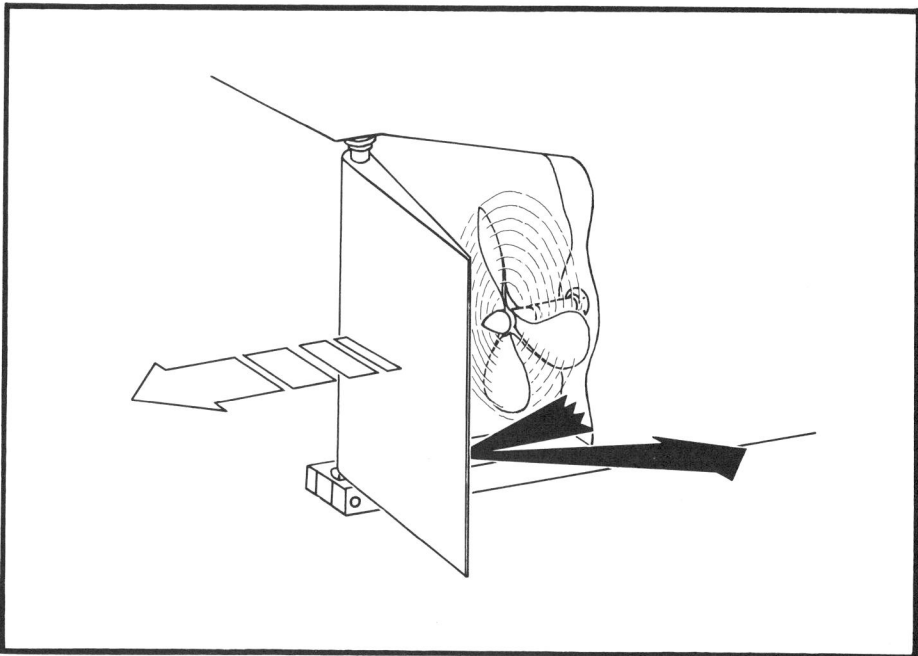

Rudder action and reaction.

nicks or roughness at their edges. If you hit a log, or go aground, it is prudent to beach the boat for an inspection and to take a piece of emery cloth to the rough edges and clean off any barnacles or slime. At the same time, inspect the space between the back of the prop and the rearmost point of the hull. It is surprising how often you will find a length of string or a piece of angler's nylon trace caught in there, and it is worrying to see how much damage it can do to rubber bushes.

Rope around the Prop

This is a perpetual anxiety, and there have been all sorts of ingenious solutions to get it off again. There are permanently

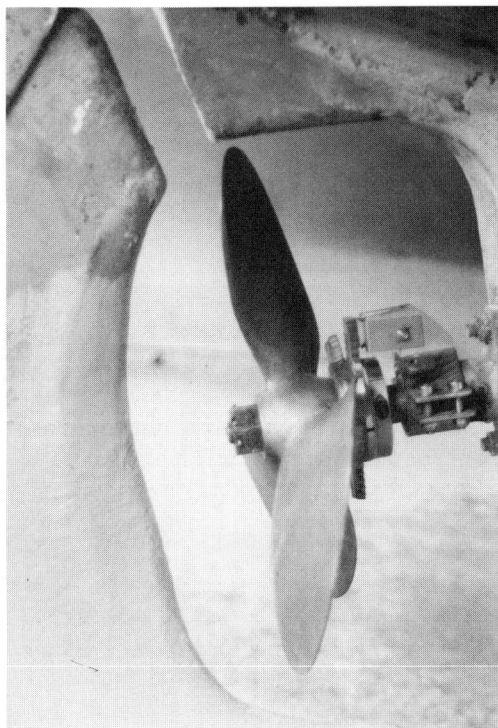

Mechanical cutters are good but not perfect.

installed mechanical cutting devices, which are very effective, but not perfect. If loose ends of rope come on at odd angles, the technology does not always cope.

After various flirtations with kitchen knives on the ends of boat hooks, we have returned to a very basic remedy for lobster-pot lines and net on the propeller. We have fitted a boarding ladder where it can be used for one of us to get low enough into the water to have a look at the problem, and it is sited so that it becomes a grab handle, or a tie-off point for a safety line, if we have to go over the side to clear the shaft.

If the sea is anything but totally calm, it will generally be necessary to use a diving mask or swimmer's goggles to see the shaft clearly under water. A snorkel tube helps, but only rarely have we needed to don full diving gear for a problem with a rope. Other crews use one of the surface supplied shallow-water breathing units. They work well.

If we are sure that the problem is weed – generally indicated by a loss of speed – we try to spin it off by putting the engine astern. If not, it is a grab and knife job. If the engine actually stops, this usually means rope. We put the gears into neutral and start the engine again, just to check that the machine will actually fire up. Having verified that important fact, we shut the motor down. Then one of us goes over the side.

Clearing net is never easy. The quickest solution is to hold it taut and to cut away all the spare, up to about 15cm (6in) from the shaft. You cannot hurry this task, which might take you half a dozen dives. Ropes merit the same treatment. Clear the debris, but leave enough to be held in one hand, both to pull off the rest when you have cut it across the blockage and to pull

Forget gadgets – nothing beats a hacksaw.

The strategically placed boarding ladder.

the diver from the surface back down to the problem.

Even though we carry a heavy-duty diving knife with a serrated edge, various experiments on our own and other people's boats have led us to abandon this in favour of a full-size hacksaw, attached to the wrist by a safety harness. The fastest way to clear rope is to pull the end as tight as you can (which also helps to keep the diver in place) and to cut diagonally across the shaft, just behind the propeller. If you are lucky, your pull will unwind much of the rope as soon as you have cut through a few strands. If not, the diagonally worked hacksaw is quite quick – even if you have the disaster of wire-cored line.

Fortunately such happenings are rare,

but cruising is coping. You manage, just as you manage your boat in typical berth situations such as the ones described below.

How these Things Work

Getting away from a quay is one of the simplest manoeuvres, yet one where you see plenty of damage done to boats. Only rarely will you have the luxury of a long, empty quay, where you can simply shove off the bow and motor straight ahead. Even this needs care. There is always the danger that a little impatience or over-enthusiasm with the rudder will crash the stern against the wall.

Even if they have this amount of room, many experienced skippers still use the standard unberthing procedure. (I have assumed no springer warps for the moment.)

To **get clear of the wall**, put the boat ahead with the bows turning into the quay.

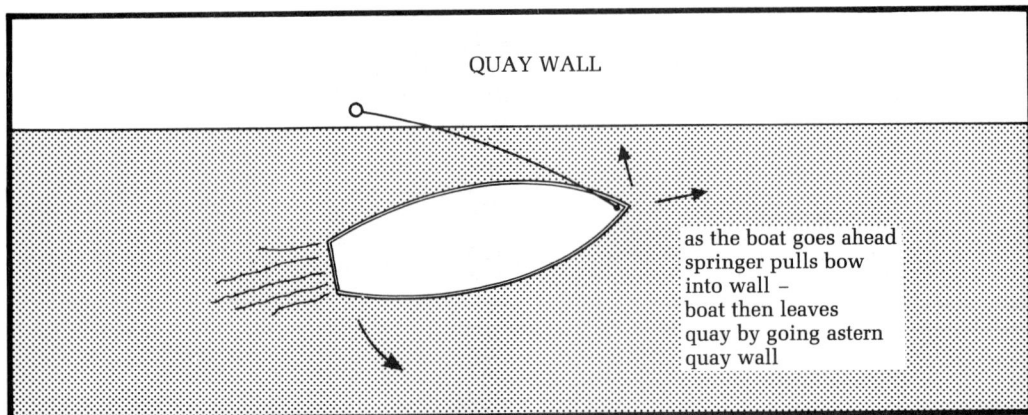

QUAY WALL

as the boat goes ahead
springer pulls bow
into wall –
boat then leaves
quay by going astern
quay wall

Using a springer to get away from a wall.

The taper of the bow leaves room to do this without collision and most boats turn sharper ahead than astern. When the boat is at an angle to the dock, put the helm amidships and come out gently astern until you are clear of all obstructions.

To **come back to the wall**, you first decide how you will be able to get away again, especially if you have to do it in a hurry. You may want your bows already facing out to sea, for example. However, in most situations, whether you are port side or starboard side to, will be decided by other factors – finger pontoon, a strong ebb tide plus estuary current, prevailing wind, etc.

As far as possible, make life easy for yourself. The flatter the angle of your approach to the berth and the earlier you can get the boat parallel to how she will finally lie – even if this means skimming close alongside the boat astern – the easier it will be to reach the final position. All of the worst coming-alongside problems are the result of being too much 'bows on' to the wall: the wind gets hold of the boat and you have to go round again, or need to get some lines rapidly ashore and begin heaving.

Other problems occur because the skipper does not know his engine, prop and rudder combination well enough, so he is reluctant to put on forward power when going ahead close to the quay. Remember that the rudder is less effective when the boat is gliding than when it has backwash from the propeller flowing over its surface. Getting into a narrow space sometimes demands a bit of verve, you drive the boat to make her turn, dwell half a second in neutral, then kick hard astern to stop her. The neutral dwell is important. It is only momentary, but it puts the reversing prop in clear water, where it gets a better grip than if it is turning in its own bubbles and disturbed water.

Authors can write for days on this topic, but the only real way to learn harbour work, once you understand the basics, is to go out and do it. Here, there is absolutely no substitute for experience.

Alternative Power

Sailing to the mooring is not seen too much nowadays – apart from picking up

It is essential to check on how your gearbox and shaft are lubricated so that you will know where to look if trouble strikes.

certain buoys – simply because our anchorages have become so crowded that the risk of damage is very high.

We shall keep our suggestions on how to use your understanding of sail power to the basics. There have been whole learned tomes written on sailing aerodynamics and sailing-hull hydrodynamics, but here is not the place for such complexity. Our task is to make cruiser management and handling as simple and easy as it can be.

The basics are that a sailing cruiser comprises a hull with mast and sails on top and a keel and ballast beneath. The upper portion provides the drive and the lower elements are designed to resist the tendency to heel and to counteract leeway – the lateral drift that a wind on one side inevitably causes. Put very simplistically, the boat cannot go sideways, so it takes the line of least resistance and goes forwards.

Most cruiser skippers have come up through dinghy racing and have a good idea of the way positive pressure on the front of the sail and negative pressure behind act exactly like an aeroplane wing, to allow the boat to go forwards.

We all also have our preferences about whether to go for a sloop (one headsail), a cutter (two headsails) or a two-masted ketch. It all comes down to whether you want the former's simplicity and efficiency up-wind, or prefer the versatility of three or four sails and the safety of handling them all from the shelter of the cockpit.

SUMMARY

- Boats are rarely travelling straight along the line of the keel.

- Both external and internal power forces are used to move the boat in many directions – some seemingly abnormal.

- Power starts the boat and stops it.

- Propellers are either left hand or right hand and walk the boat's stern accordingly.

- A prop is always stamped with its diameter and pitch. These control acceleration and speed.

- Do you know your boat prop's operating characteristics? How does your prop kick? Ahead? Astern?

- The correct prop for the boat needs research. If you get it wrong you create extra wear, tear and expense.

- A clean prop with sharp edges is an efficient prop.

- If you plan a new engine, you might also need a new gearbox. If you neglect the boring job of turning down the grease gland regularly you might soon need a new prop shaft and gearbox.

- A hacksaw is a very desirable safety tool.

2

THE CRUISER MANAGERS

In proper cruising, the crew are just as important as the boat they manage. Whilst it is true that a good boat will often forgive a poor crew and even keep them out of trouble, it is also true that a good crew will work wonders with a poor boat and miracles with a good one.

How many people you actually need to crew your cruiser depends on a number of factors. Bigger boats obviously require more people to handle them, but doubling the boat size does not necessarily mean having twice as many hands on board. Cruisers, who are rarely in a hurry and mostly able to pick their weather, can generally manage with minimum personnel.

Our own boat has berths for four or five people, but when we are asked about this we confess only to two and rarely have more than this number aboard. Even on passages lasting three or four days continuously, we find that we are able to cope. During the day, we are both loosely on the alert but if one of us decides to read, or to go below, we simply tell the other 'you have the boat'. From 2200 to 0800 we work two-hour watches, with only one of us in the wheel-house. This system is not universal but it suits us and our way of doing things. More gregarious boat owners like to have plenty of people about them and

either to have two people awake to share each night watch, or to have an overlapping two- or three-hour system giving longer and deeper periods of proper sleep and a bit of company to share the dark.

All owners and boats are different, but there are a number of fundamental precepts to cruising and crews. They are best illustrated by the comments of the skipper of a very tidy Halberg Rassey who anchored near us in Spain a couple of years ago. As so often happens, we ended up with an impromptu, late-evening party in the cockpit of one boat or another, talking about cruising boats, cruises and cruising people. On all these topics, John evinced considerable wisdom.

Cruising Success or Failure?

'We have met very many people who eventually realize the dream which they have been working towards for a number of years. They have bought the boat of their choice and have made arrangements about their shore-side properties and are finally able to set off to follow the sun for three or four years. Within twelve months of leaving home, a surprising number of them have abandoned the project, probably

VARIOUS CREWS GIVE DIFFERENT NIGHT WATCHES

Two person crew gets 2 on and 2 off

Four person crew has 2 on and 2 off, but a change of companion every hour

Six person crew can have 3 on and 6 off to get a long sleep

Possible watchkeeping schemes compared.

had to leave the boat to rot somewhere like the Caribbean and they are back at their desks. This will generally be for one of three reasons.

'Firstly, they have planned the venture badly, so they run out of money. Cruising is surprisingly cheap once you have a good yacht and its gear, but you still need an adequate budget for boat, berthing, food and contingency against breakage. Running out of money means that they did not sufficiently talk it through amongst themselves, nor did they discuss the project with people who have already done it and who would be able to give them some realistic figures and counsel. Some people, for instance, set off with vaguely optimistic plans about earning money whilst they are out. Then they come up against local work-permit laws and native resentment. You have to be a specialist, like a marine electronics expert, to have any chance of earning money whilst cruising.

'Secondly, they find that they were perfectly well matched when he had his career and she either had her own job or ran the household. At home, they probably had their own hobbies and interests and had something different to talk about over dinner.

'Aboard a 25–40-foot (7.5–12-metre) yacht, all day and every day, it is a very different story. There is no way that you can avoid the other people in the crew and you inevitably do absolutely everything together. Suddenly, our couple find that they are not as well matched as they previously believed, so they become bored with each other's company, often get a bit tetchy and they scurry off back home.

'Thirdly, some people buy a boat which is too big for them. It scares them witless when they have all the canvas up and she is tearing along in a blow. They dare not go into the best marina berths, nor enter those super-tiny harbours, because they

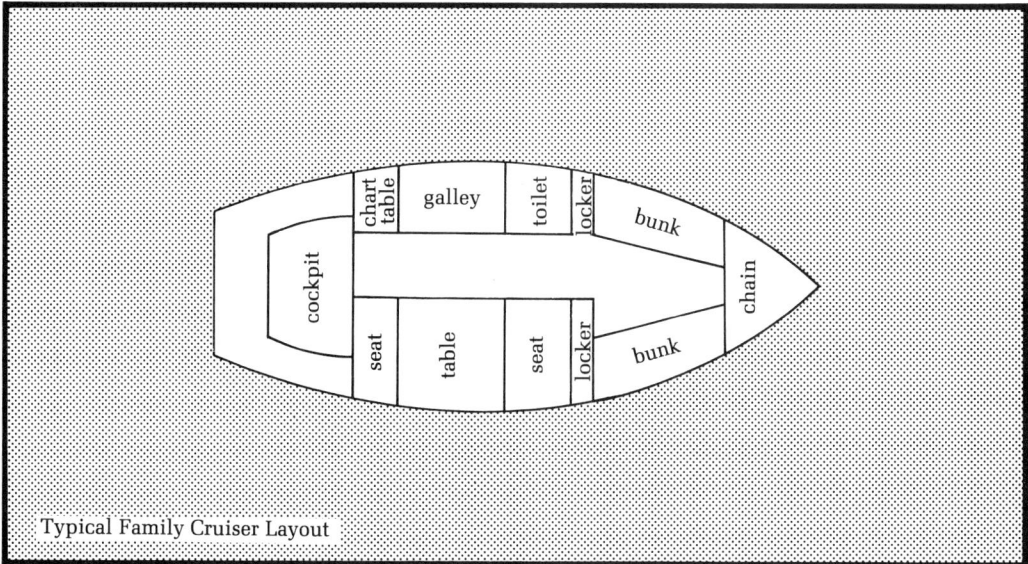

Typical Family Cruiser Layout

On a standard family cruiser, this is all the space you have for eating, sleeping and living.

If the crew is well balanced, each one gets some time to relax.

that people who have spent a long time going over their cruise-plan time and time again with each other, plus discussing it with club members who know each other and their boats, will have a greater chance of being a good crew.

The Ideal Boat Crew

The perfect boat crew probably does not exist, but many experienced couples get close to the ideal. Their efficiency comes – yes – with experience, but also because they have worked the boat with each other for long enough to have evolved a handling system that suits them. In simple, everyday situations such as docking, undocking and anchoring, such a crew will communicate perfectly adequately with little or no need to speak.

At other times, there will be a long planning talk. A typical example from our own log happened this past season. We had spent the night tucked behind a harbour wall, but swinging about on our own anchor. There were no waves, but we did have more than forty-knots of wind at times, so we kept an anchor watch, i.e. all through the night; one of us was awake in the wheel-house to monitor the instruments we needed and above all to keep an eye on the shore marks. Abeam, we had a couple of street lamps exactly in line and, as long as they stayed that way, we were not dragging.

cannot completely handle a boat of that size. These are often people who have suddenly acquired enough cash and are actually realizing their long-term cruising dream in the very first boat they have ever owned – and it is one which they are not well enough experienced to run properly.

'A better system is to do a bit of coastal cruising to sort out your personal strengths and weaknesses and those of your crew, however many they are, then you will more likely get a combination which suits you.'

It is significant that all of John's reasons for failure are due to the interaction of people with each other. The opposite is

Come the dawn, the wind was down to an average thirty-five knots, so we decided to move into more shelter and safety alongside the quay, which was very new and not yet complete, so it was absolutely empty. It was also about 7.5m (25ft) high and accessed by a single, narrow ladder between stout bollards about 23m (75ft)

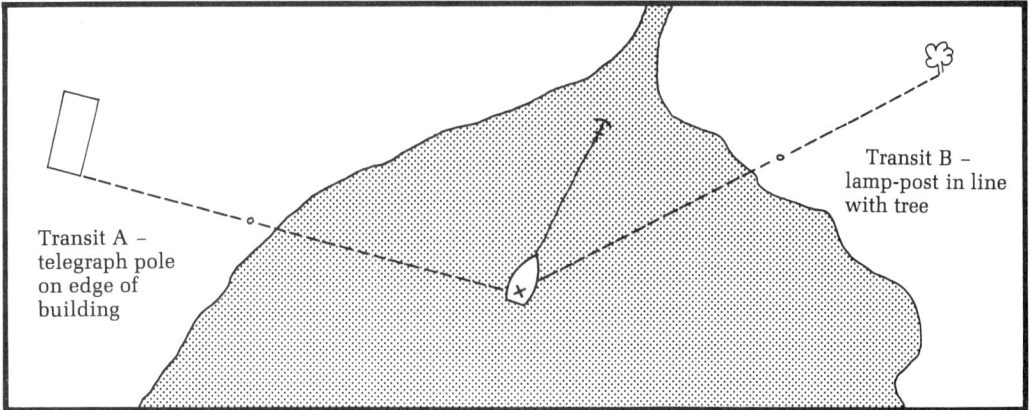

Using shore transits to keep anchor station.

apart. Going starboard side to the wall would put the nose directly into the wind, so we rigged the fenders.

The plan was for the lady of the crew to go up the ladder with our two longest ropes, into which large, looped bowlines were already tied. The other ends of the ropes were left free – one on the foredeck and one snaking out of the cockpit. If the wind really got between the bow of the boat and the wall and blasted her away from the quay, there was no danger that the climber would be pulled off the ladder. It did not appear to be the easiest of tasks.

Equally, if she could get a loop over the forward bollard, it could be made fast on board with a couple of turns round the anchor capstan, then the helmsman could dash back to the wheel-house and ease the boat astern, to tighten this line and to hold her on to the wall whilst the after line was secured. Alternately, if the first rope had to be put onto the bollard astern of the boat, she could be held to the wall by

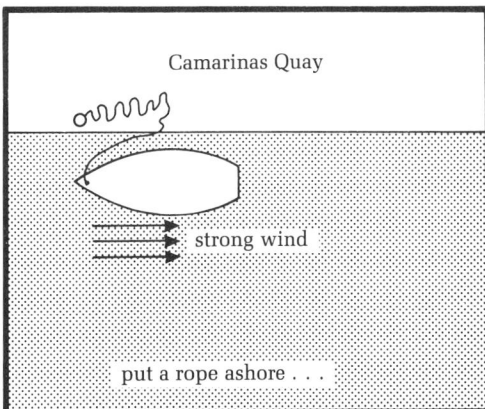

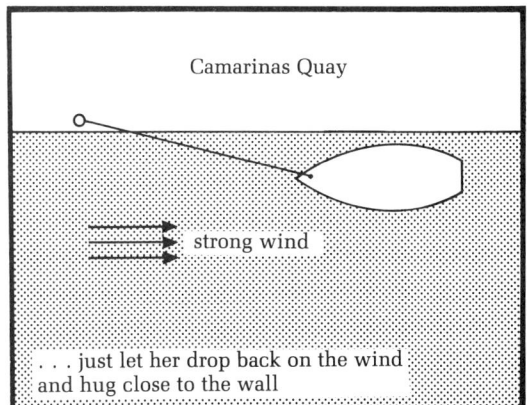

With one warp ashore, let her drop back on the wind.

going firmly ahead with the wheel set into the quay and pinning the boat against her fenders for the brief period that would be needed to get the second warp in place.

If it all went wrong, we should at least have one person on shore with two long ropes, which could eventually be made fast anywhere on the boat, if the wind won the first stage of the contest and we were forced to pay off and come round again.

The manoeuvre went like clockwork, with the engine holding the boat against the fenders for the climb, then disengaged whilst the helmsman made a trip to the foredeck to make the first rope fast, before allowing the boat to drop back on this secured bow warp. Because we had talked it through thoroughly and had discussed a series of 'what if' scenarios, we both knew what we had to do. So it worked.

That is probably the nub of good crewing. Bad crews are short on seamanship knowledge and compound this by insufficient on-board communication with each other, so that nobody completely understands what is happening. Charter crews, with too many skippers and insufficient deckhands, are especially prone to this malaise.

A wheel-house boat has plenty to be learned.

great deal of discussion on our own boats and cruises, and will partially achieve its purpose if it does the same on yours.

The Need to Know

There are a certain number of essentials that all members of the crew should understand. This is not to say that all passengers should be skilled in every quirk of navigation and pilotage, but, if anyone is helping to run the ship, the basic facts of certain boat situations should be familiar.

The syllabus below is derived from discussions with a good number of experienced skippers. It is not claimed to be perfect, but it has certainly engendered a

How the Boat Works

Every crew member should be able to understand boat language – sheets, shackles, heads and other common terms. The learning curve is made easier if the skipper does not hog things, but gives everybody a turn at steering the boat on the compass, engaging and disengaging the autopilot, taking readings from all of the instruments and writing the log. All hands should help with getting sails on and off and setting them. Everybody should be nominally in charge of the boat for a time (chief watchkeeper) even if only under supervision. All crew members should know a fair amount about the safety aids, fire extinguishers and flares. Each one should be able to light and use the cooker and to locate the first-aid kit.

Basic Seamanship

This needs no more than the ability to tie a bowline and a round turn and two half hitches. Many skippers go their whole lives with no more than these basic knots, which both have the virtue of getting tighter under stress, but being easy to undo (even with wet ropes) when the tension is removed.

Navigation

This becomes more interesting if crew members can recognize the major chart features, can plot a latitudinal and longitudinal position, and know how to step off distances with the dividers. These basics alone make any person a very useful watchkeeper and let everyone have the fun of doing some plotting whenever they feel like amusing themselves.

Pilotage mark spotting is an essential crew function. When the going gets really tricky, a skipper can never have too many pairs of assistant eyes, especially if they know what they are looking for. Then they will not confuse the day by calling attention to irrelevancies.

Who needs more? Bowline and round turn and two half hitches.

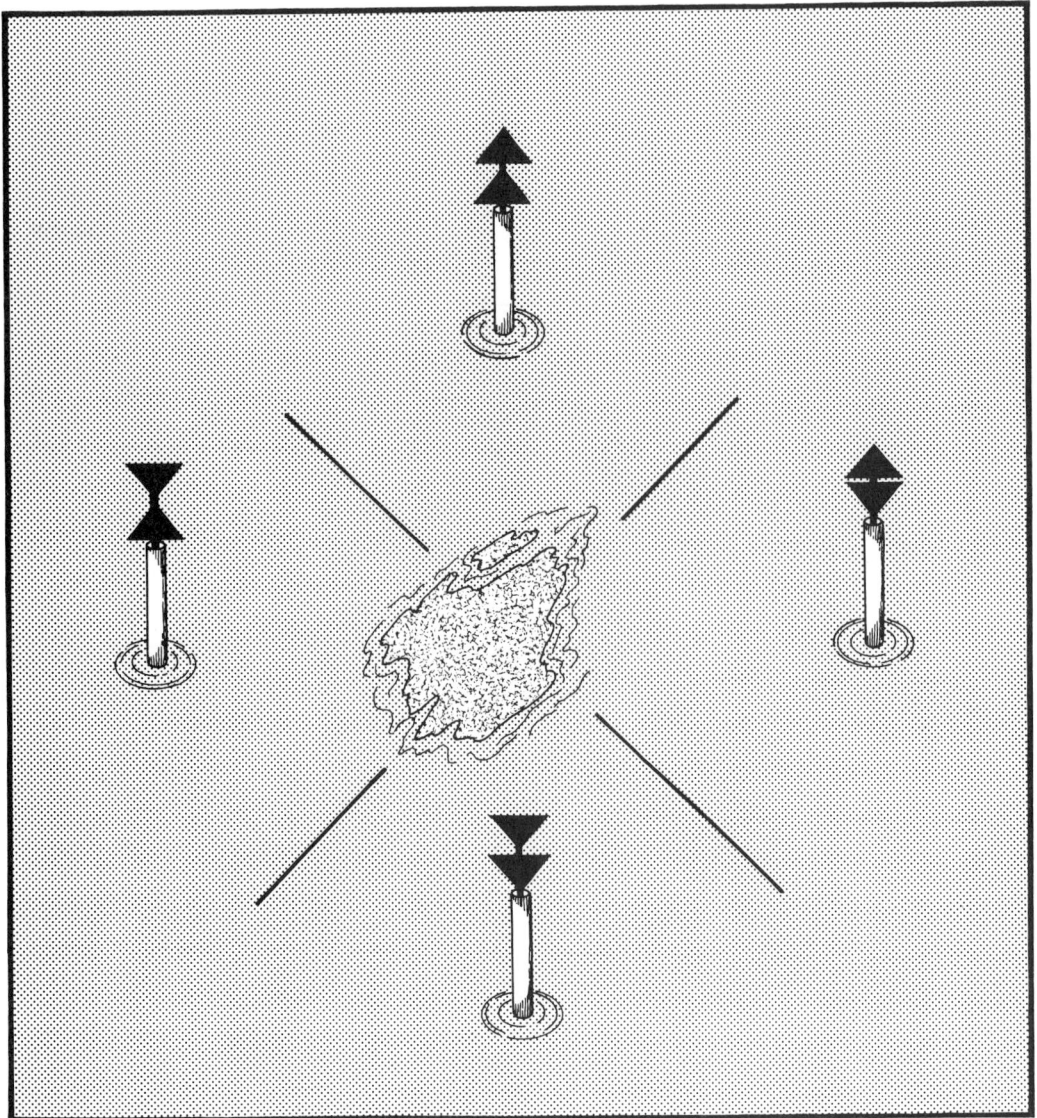

The crew should be able to recognize the most important marks.

The basic needs are to recognize the colours and shapes of channel and harbour port, starboard, isolated danger and safe water marks and also to recognize the topmarks and (to a lesser extent) the colours of IALA buoyage cardinal N E S W marks.

The fundamental **Rules of the Road** and **Common Navigation Lights** are also useful knowledge to have, even if they are only

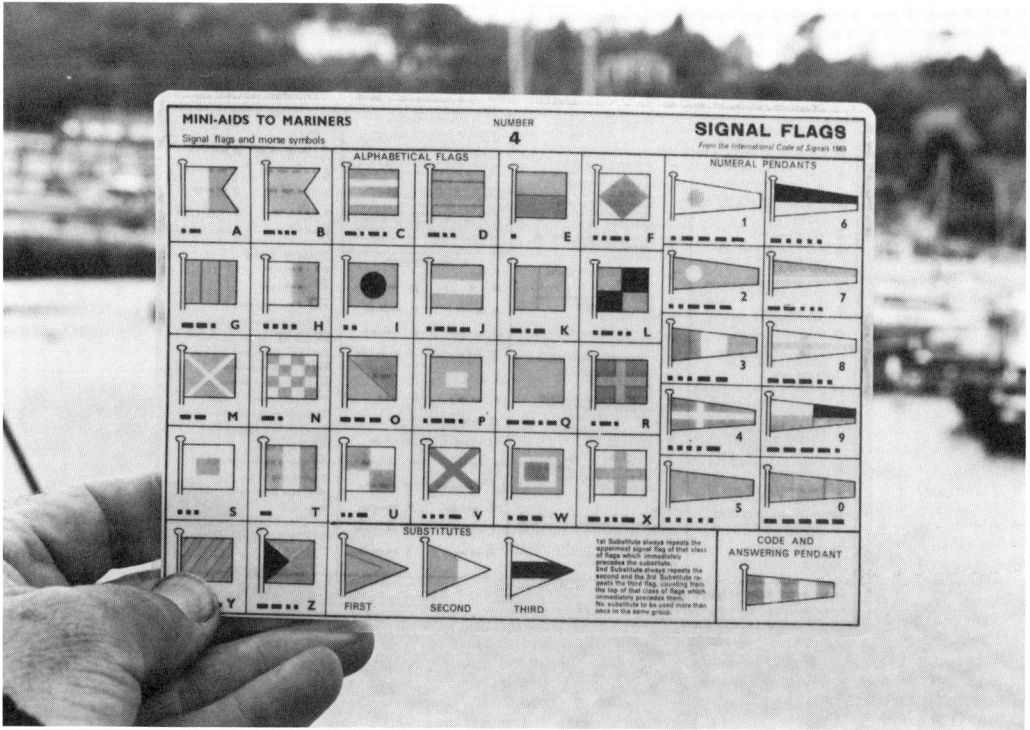

There are some excellent on-board *aide-mémoires* for unusual lights and marks.

Skipper or manager? A small part of our summer cruise bill of lading.

used to be able to understand why the skipper is taking this action or that in relation to other vessels, or to patterns of light at night.

Part of the fun of cruising and also of cruise planning, with beginners and with newcomers to your boat, is that they acquire this knowledge, from the more experienced, bit by bit as time goes along. Once they have the basics in the curriculum above, they are very useful crew members to have around. In fact, they do not need much more, other than plenty of boat-handling practice, to become skippers in their own right.

Skippers? Or managers? There is much more to owning a boat than just driving it out and back. Soon they will be in the world of anti-fouling, locating fuel supplies, ordering charts, arranging the larder, collecting up the spares and so many more things that they will soon see a cruising boat not so much as a summertime marine caravan, but as a total, totally absorbing, year-round hobby.

SUMMARY

- In cruise crewing, smaller numbers often mean more efficiency.

- Before planning a long cruise, examine both self and companions. Can you be compatible for long periods?

- Do you know how much it will cost per day to live in your cruise area?

- The big error: a boat which is too big for its crew.

- Every manoeuvre should be talked through with the whole crew before its execution. Every knows what everybody else is doing.

- All crew members should be assistant navigators. It is a mistake for the skipper to keep the mystique for himself.

- All crew should know the major marks and lights.

- Have reference cards at the steering position.

- If you became ill, could your crew get the boat home?

- Remember, you are not a commander but a boat manager.

3
LET'S GO TO SEA

Any discussion of handling boats on an actual cruise must start with what might appear to some skippers to be a very low threshold of fundamentals. However, discussions around the club bar will often show up a number of owners who have not the faintest idea of what sort of boat they have purchased, nor what the designer had in mind when he sketched it out on his drawing board. Alas, the result is often the disappointment of a family who have mistakenly bought a river boat, when they would now really prefer to be going across the Channel.

In knowing boats, there really is absolutely no substitute for driving them for a few hours – better still, a few days. When the yacht is in purely motoring mode, a

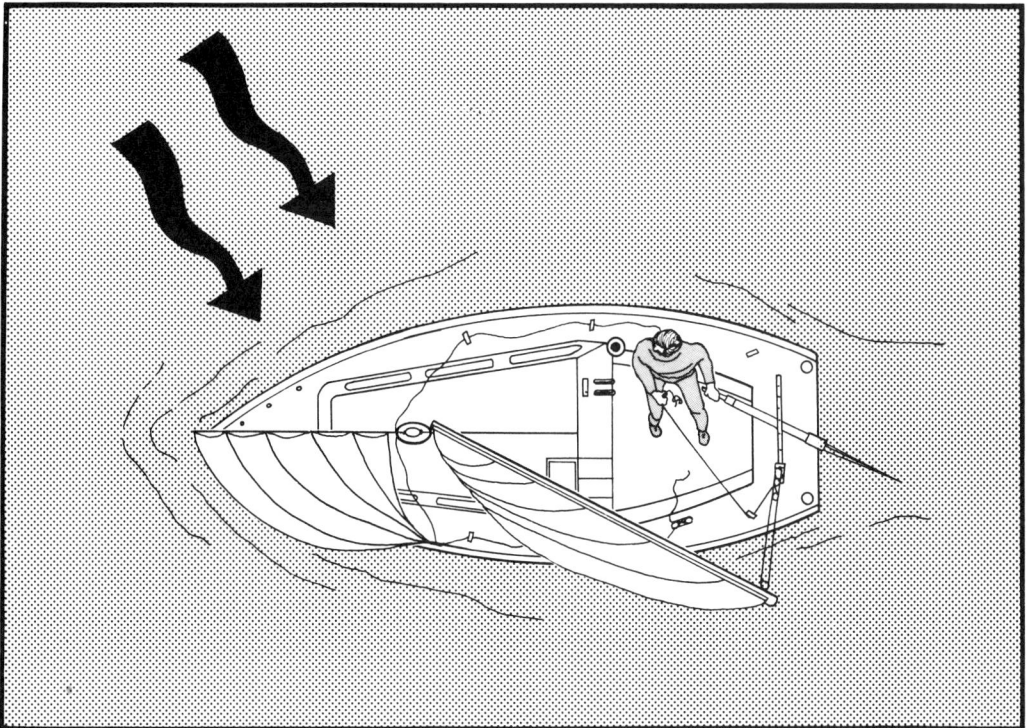

Will go up-wind very badly.

whole multitude of sins can be covered up and will be compensated for by adequate engine power, allied with firm handling. It is under sail – and even when motor sailing – that the boat's true performance over the period of a cruise will show up and it will largely be dictated by the characteristics of the hull and further influenced by the way she is rigged.

Put in very simple terms, a hull that looks like a trawler, with a wide beam, a cabin with full headroom and a sheer up to a high bow, will give a dry, slow, ride. She will go up-wind very badly and you might even need to start the engine to get her onto the other tack. Off the wind, she will go as well as most others.

The slim, 'Dragon'-style racer, or part-time cruiser, with a very fine, wave-cutting bow, an overhung stern and not very much freeboard from deck down to water-line, will be a real flier. She will have either a lifting keel or a deep keel and this will assist very rapid up-wind tacking. The trade-off is that the crew will get soaked and the accommodation will be cramped.

In some schools of thought, there is now a discernible preference for cruiser-racers, which can be used for club racing 'around the cans' and for family holidays. It is giving rise to such complaints as 'All French boats look alike'. The hull is shallow and rounded until it turns flat and hard into the keel. These boats are usually beamy right to the transom. Downwind

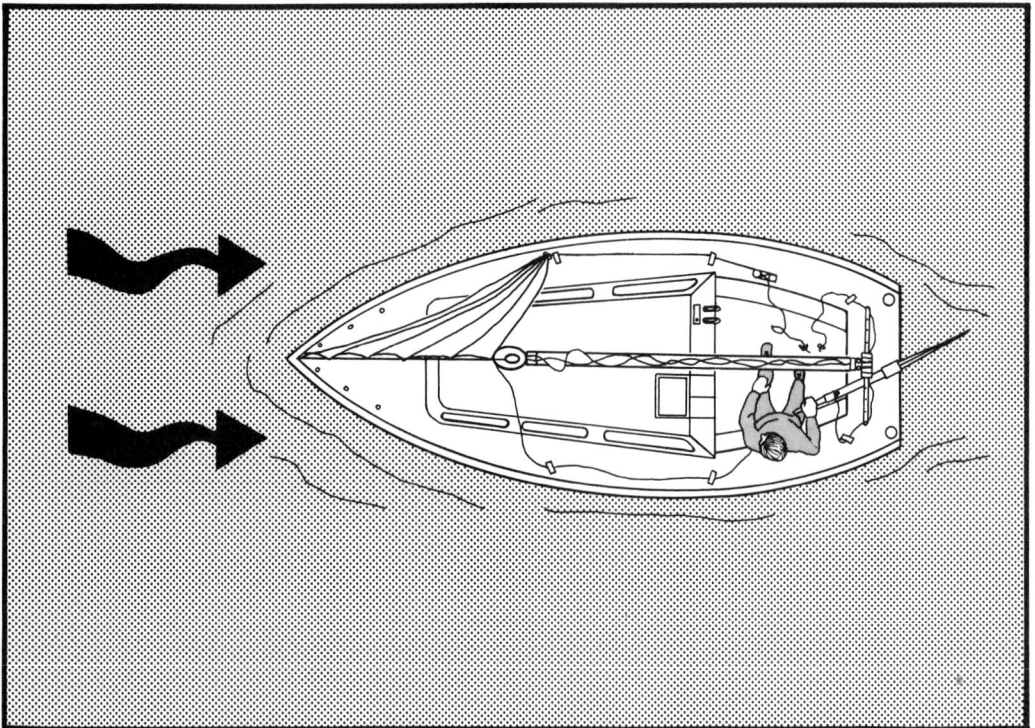

You need a slimline for speed.

The distinctive shape of the motor sailer. This Colvic Watson 28 foot ketch is creaming along under full sail.

A smaller day sailing boat, ideal for the family who, when they don't want to carry on sailing, can simply start the outboard engine and cruise under power.

A nippy cruiser sailer with cabin for two. This boat has a simple Bermuda rig of a single main and jib. A small outboard provides auxiliary power.

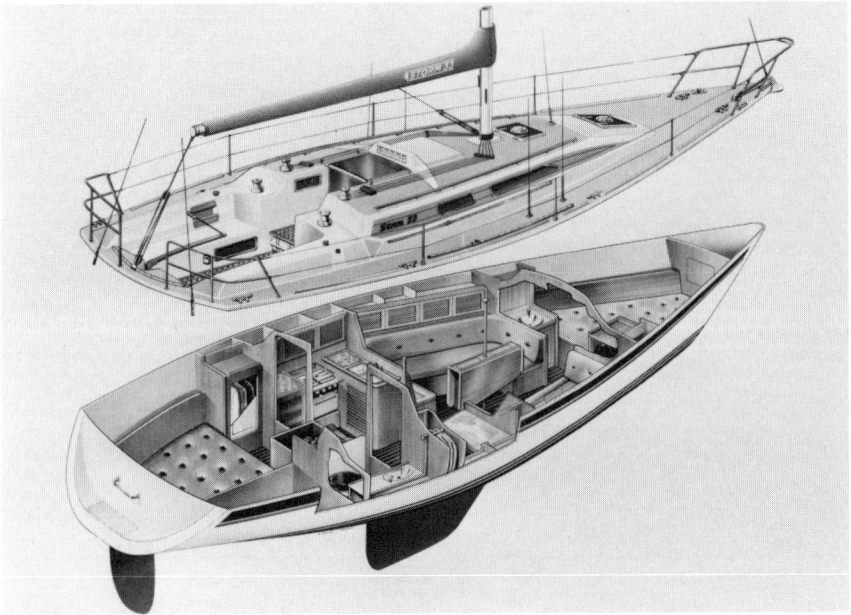

A cutaway of a 33ft luxury sailing cruiser designed for serious ocean-going voyages. This Storm 33 features a cruiser interior with three double cabins.

they really fly. Up-wind they are adequate, but require plenty of weight up the weather side to balance them properly.

In between these extremes are many variations, each having its slight effect on how the boat handles. You can learn how she will cruise only by going out in her. Most of us, however, have a 'gut' feeling about the sort of boat we want, even before we go looking seriously. In spite of this, you really must demand a full sea trial of any boat on your short list. Politeness does not pay in this situation, in which you will be spending at least the value of a car and possibly the equivalent of a house. So, out and back is not good enough. You want to see how you will be able to handle the boat on all points of sail and in all situations. You need to go through a month's cruise in half a day, in order to check that you and the boat can do what should be done together.

Weather Helm

A boat that does not want to come up into the wind is badly out of balance. With the wind anywhere forward of the quarter, it should be necessary to pull the tiller a bit up to windward, or to take a tension on the the wheel, to keep the boat's head on a straight line and away from the wind. This phenomenon brings a few advantages.

1 The boat will tack more quickly, because she always wants to go that way and will round up very fast, just as soon as you let the weather helm off.
2 This is also a safety factor. If something goes wrong, or you spot a lobster pot at the last moment, you know that the boat will fly into stays, head to wind and come to a halt just as soon as you let go of the tiller.

The same would happen if you had a cockpit accident and released the tiller in the process.
3 It makes gybing and other turns that swing the stern of the boat through the wind much more under control.

Heaving to

Stopping a sailing boat and balancing her so that she stays at rest, without paying off on one tack or the other, is normally thought of as a bad-weather technique. In fact, many skippers facing severe weather, prefer to let the boat lie a-hull under bare poles, but still practise heaving to. It can be a useful skill when you are crossing shipping lanes and want to stop to let a cargo vessel pass ahead of you, or so that you can reduce the lookout whilst you go below to make a cup of tea.

The simplest technique is to sail as close hauled as possible, even pinching the nose tight into the wind, but keeping minimum steerage way. Then tack the boat, but leave the jib sheets cleated hard home. Do the same with the mainsail and she should stay head to wind. She is kept there by the boat's natural tendency to point up into the wind, resisted by the action of the 'backed jib' trying to force the head away from it. Heaving to is a matter of getting the forces balanced against each other.

This manoeuvre will fail if your headsail is too large, or has too much genoa balloon in its shape. It is easiest to do with a ketch, whose mizzen resists the stern's tendency to get across the wind. Whichever way the stern tries to get off line, the hard-sheeted, flat plane of the mizzen will attempt to push it back.

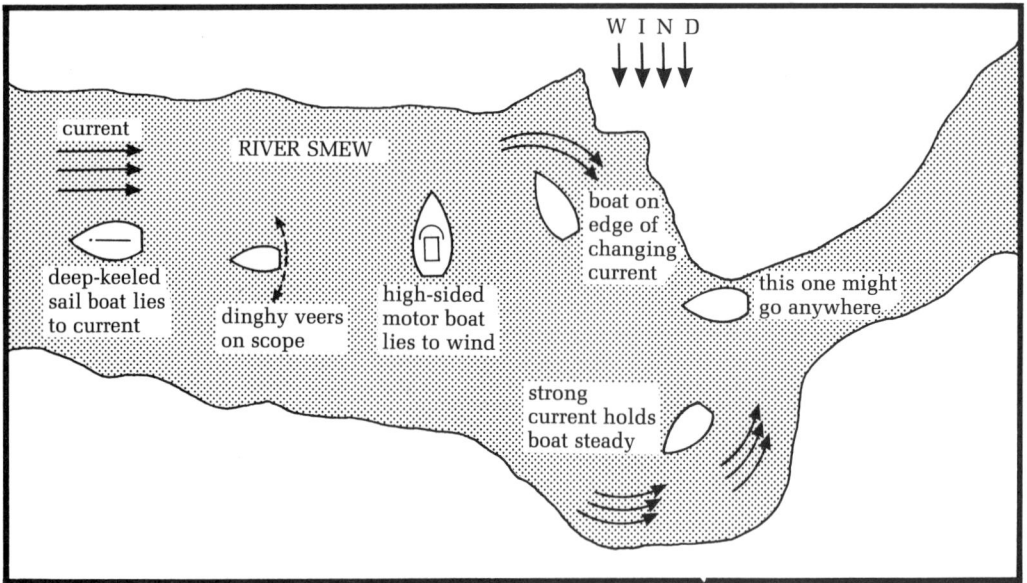

Left to themselves, all boats lie differently.

Lying Athwart

Also try the boat with all sheets slackened off so far that the sails can blow out at right angles to the line of the hull. Some boats will stay broadside to the wind: others – such as our own – will let the bow drop off and will try to lie stern to the wind. A boat that will stay athwart the wind, whilst the crew sorts out a tangle, is easier to manage than ours.

Reefing

Shortening sail happens to us all and not all of us can afford in-mast furling. There are others who dislike the shape that the system gives to a partly reefed sail, and are not happy with the reduced efficiency that is created by a sail disappearing inside the mast housing.

Like many cruising boats, our motor sailer has slab, or jiffy, reefing, which is quick and simple. Our down-pull cords are not led back to the cockpit, but we always reeve their lines through the eyes in the back edge of the sail ready for immediate pull-down to the boom. Some skippers are content to have the reefed sail made fast only at the mast and at the end of the boom, with the spare sail pouched and flogging, but we have been discouraged by the noise of the loose canvas, which might last for days on end, plus the thought of damage as canvas beats against canvas and the boom.

These days, we prefer to thread a bungy, shock cord through the four reefing points in the sail itself and to pull it all down snug, secure, tidy, not flapping, tight to the boom.

Roller Reefing Headsails

It is rare that you see a serious cruising sailing boat without a roller reefing headsail. Whilst it is true that the mechanism does not create the best pulling shape, when the sail is partly furled and it shifts the centre of effort higher above the centre of gravity, the pluses outnumber the minuses.

In heavy weather, we spend many hours running on just mizzen and genoa. We can work both sails, shorten them and can even stow both without needing to leave the safety of the cockpit.

Probably the ideal set-up is a couple of good, pulling sails that are cut to fit into the furling headsail mechanism's groove, plus a second forestay onto which normal,

We spend a lot of time under mizzen and genoa.

flat, up-wind sails can be hanked with standard clips. This would give a sloop the headsail versatility of the cutter – with the security of a second, masthead, wire stay thrown in for good measure.

Single-Sail Handling

There will also be times when it is more convenient to set just one sail. Most boats will handle tolerably well on either the mainsail or a headsail. It pays to try both and to fiddle about a bit to see what really happens to performance when you are single-sail driven.

Many boats with a masthead-rigged genoa handle better on that alone than with the mainsail set on its own. We have certain angles at which the mainsail inter-feres so badly with our biggest genoa that dropping the main altogether actually causes the boat to increase speed. This is especially noticeable in light airs.

Final Examination

I would never contemplate buying a sailing cruiser unless the seller was willing to show all the characteristics above to me and also to let me sail her on all points of the wind. When you get out away from the shore, these are the things that you and the boat will have to do.

Sometimes, you will be required to do these things very rapidly and under pressure. It is comforting to know, right from the pre-purchase days, that you are both able to cope.

SUMMARY

- River boats should stay on rivers. At sea they become dangerous. Is the boat suitable for your location?

- You can have fast boats, sea boats and load carriers but cannot have all these attributes in a single hull.

- Weather helm is not dangerous unless it is excessive.

- The wind is the best boat driver and the best boat stopper.

- Take some reefs in on a calm day.

- Do you know if your boat would manoeuvre on a single sail?

- Generally speaking, if you cannot try you should not buy.

- Before you buy add in the running costs – berthing, fuel, insurance, winter storage and upkeep – just for a start.

- If a boat looks good to you, she will probably feel good and you will probably make her behave well too.

- Seamanship is a duality. Good boat plus good skipper in tune.

4

ANCHORING – THE FORGOTTEN ART

Anchoring has almost become the lost art in a cruising scene that is increasingly dominated by marinas. This is not to decry the present situation. Its only major drawback is the very high cost of berthing, especially to the serious, long-term cruiser looking for many days a year. A minor minus is also that marinas are rarely sited in those very beautiful places where you can wake to a warming sun and the seabirds calling to each other on the shore, so we miss part of the fun when we are forced into using them.

If you want to enjoy your boat to the full and to be able to go to sleep with total peace of mind, you need to be able to anchor your boat and to be 95 per cent certain that the anchor will hold. You would – likewise – be very fortunate indeed to pass through your entire cruising life without the need to use the anchor in one of the semi-emergency situations, such as grounding or getting a rope around the prop.

So, like it or not, anchoring is still a skill that is an essential part of being a competent cruising skipper and having it may even be the difference between losing your boat and saving her.

Which Anchor?

It is almost certain that your new cruising boat will be delivered with the minimum anchor and warp required to meet national body recommendations and to cover normal insurance requirements. When you add all your cruising crew and their gear, plus spares, fuel, water and food, you may find that you are a bit short on holding power.

The reasons for this minimum delivery specification are cost and stowage, which are the same reasons for the dilemmas faced by an owner buying a new anchor. He must trust it: but at the same time he has to be able to stow it where it is not dangerous to feet, where it can be reached quickly and where it does not upset the balance or the appearance of the yacht.

The style of anchor(s) that you choose is as much a matter of pure prejudice as of effectiveness. All anchors are a compromise, with none of them being universally perfect for every type of holding ground. The most usual types seen on cruising boats, these days, seem to be the Bruce, CQR (abbreviated form of SECURE) and Danforth (or Meon) types.

The Bruce is very efficient in mud, but is inclined to roll in sand. It is a real brute to stow in spite of its excellent ratio of light

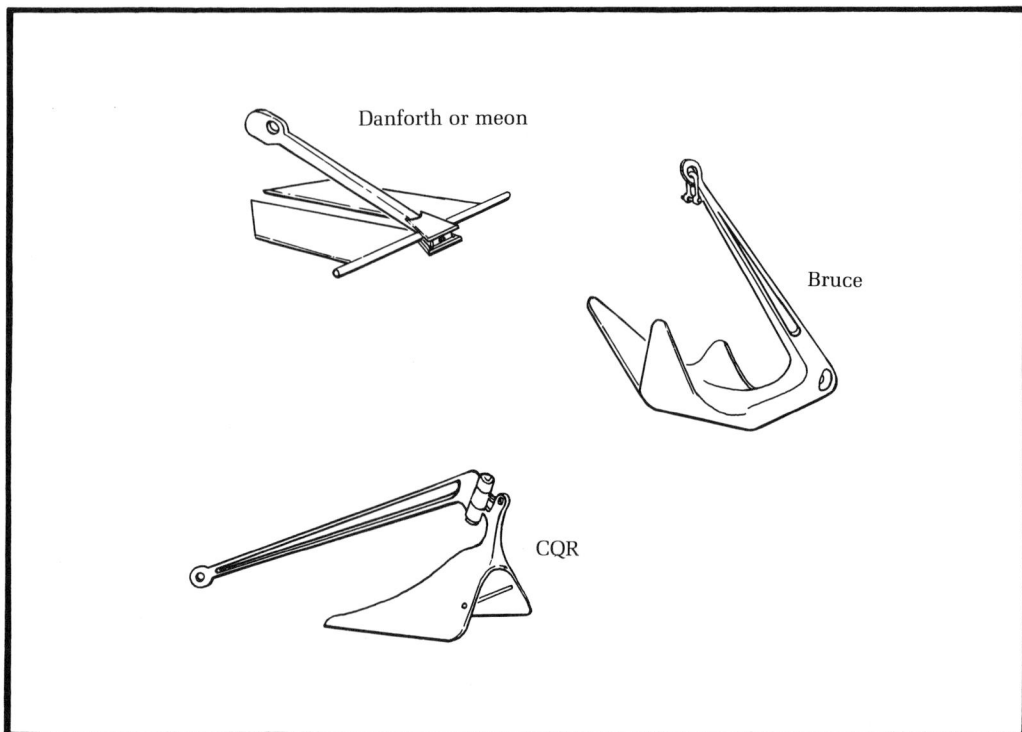

Danforth or meon

Bruce

CQR

There are various styles of anchor.

weight to holding power. The CQR's swivel makes it a little easier to stow, but it is generally heavier for the same boat. The Danforth falls in between the two for weight and is top of the league for easy stowage, but its holding power in firm ground is a bit suspect.

Recently, there have been a couple of newcomers. Amongst these, the American Fortress is worth looking at, because of its rave reviews and good results from tests, but also because it can be dismantled for long-passage stowing. Another virtue is the ability to set the flukes at the best angle to suit the ground they have to dig into. That is the sort of versatility that a cruising boat will always find useful.

A tour of 100 boats berthed in Cherbourg's Chantereyne marina listed 52 CQRs, 27 Danforths, 12 Bruce plus nine assorted others amongst main anchors. Our own boat weighs 7.5 tonnes (7.4 tons) and is served by a 16kg (35lb) CQR and 16kg (35lb) Fortress as main anchors, with a 7kg (15lb) CQR as a stern holder, a kedge or a picnic anchor.

The popularity of the CQR undoubtedly derives from its effectiveness in a wide range of undersea terrains. If it is properly set up, it will get a good hold in most types of ground. As the wind and tide cause the boat to circle around her anchor, it inevitably breaks out for a moment. The best hooks are those that immediately dig in again. Dives to a CQR anchor have revealed an encouraging trace pattern of

Current RYA Recommended Anchor Weights

LOA	Anchor weight		Anchor cable diameter			
	main	kedge	main chain rope		kedge chain rope	
metres	kg	kg	mm	mm	mm	mm
Up to 9	15	8	8	12	6	10
10	17	9	8	14	8	12
11	20	10	8	14	8	12
12	23	12	8	14	8	12
13	26	13	9·5	16	8	12
14	30	15	9·5	16	8	14

roll and resettle. That, plus our experiences in very strong winds, give us good confidence in it – and that is worth plenty.

However, if you use your anchor but rarely and only then in settled weather, you would be as well suited by one of the easy stowage models. A long-term cruising boat will always need two, so you may choose to go for one of each.

Even the official recommendation (*see* table above) can be taken only as an approximate guide, because it is based purely on length and ignores such extra pulling forces as weight, beam and windage.

The Warp

An anchor cannot be divorced from whatever connects it to the boat – generally rope, chain, or a mixture of the two.

Rope should always be some sort of nylon, which will stretch and 'give' as the boat tugs to her anchor in waves and strong gusts of wind. This elasticity reduces the 'snatch' effect, which is likely to jerk the anchor from the pit that it has dug for itself and is much kinder to the tie-off point on board.

Chain has the advantage of weight and a high degree of resistance to chafe, both on the sea-bed and at the stemhead. Ideally, all anchors should be chain held, because of the increased catenation effect – that physical phenomenon that brings the warp from anchor to bow in a curve, which very often decelerates the pull of the boat to a gentle tug on the anchor, or absorbs all of the strain along its own length.

Because chain is expensive, bulky and heavy, many skippers opt for the compromise of a length of chain, which runs along the seabed, spliced to a length of the heaviest duty nylon (or similar) that they can afford and can stow. A general-purpose combination is 9m (30ft) of chain onto 45m (148ft) of 10–20mm (0.4–0.8in) plaited rope.

Our own boat is typical of many longer-distance cruisers, which might spend a couple of weeks anchored on the same berth. In some French and Spanish harbours, for instance, you not only save £10 plus per night by being 'on the hook', but you are out where it is less noisy, where the boat is less likely to be vandalized and there is more to see and to do. We are currently equipped with the CQR (as already described) and with the Fortress on the chain/rope combination above, plus the kedge or stern anchor on 9m (30ft) of chain and whatever stretchy rope comes out of our abundant cordage locker. However, the most frequently used CQR is on 40m

The catenation effect.

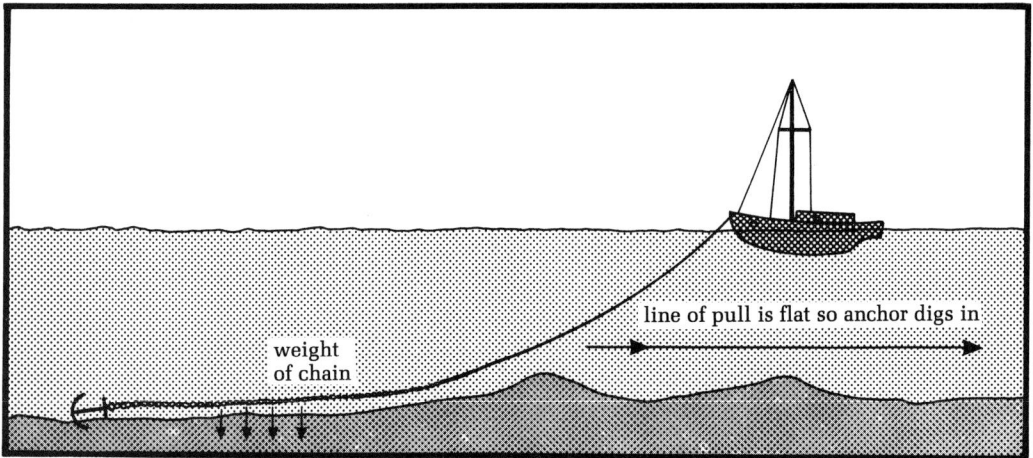

line of pull is flat so anchor digs in

weight
of chain

How chain helps to keep pull flat.

(131ft) of 10mm (0.4in) galvanized chain, with another 30m (98ft) available for heavy blows and special circumstances. After this we have a further 50m (165ft) of adequate rope, which can be used doubled, should life become really hairy and scary.

There are no hard-and-fast rules here. Anchors and anchoring will always be a source of debate and personal preference amongst cruising people. There is no perfect, universal solution, so you just have to heed all of the advice from the pundits, then buy and try what seems to be the best for your kind of boat and how you use it. A belt-and-braces, overkill philosophy is best, because that will let you sleep most soundly. When the chips are down, I am quite happy to be kept awake by the thought of all that heavy chain groaning away down there where the maximum weight you can muster is really one of the two best defences against drag that you can have.

Setting the Anchor

Choosing the spot where you will actually drop your anchor is almost as brain bending and time-consuming as buying the wretched thing. Like most crews, we prowl around a strange port weighing up its prevailing conditions and trying to get the best compromise for holding ground, shelter from wind and strongest tides, protection from waves and the wash of other boats, reasonably short access to a landing place, plus avoiding certain hills and buildings in order to have the sun in the cockpit for most of the day.

The holding ground will usually be Hobson's Choice. The area might be all sand or mud. However, many of the most sheltered and picturesque anchorages are a mixture of sand, rock and clumps of weed, where it is essential to drop the pick into one of the sandy patches. Fortunately, you can usually spot these by the changes in water colour, but the de-luxe solution is

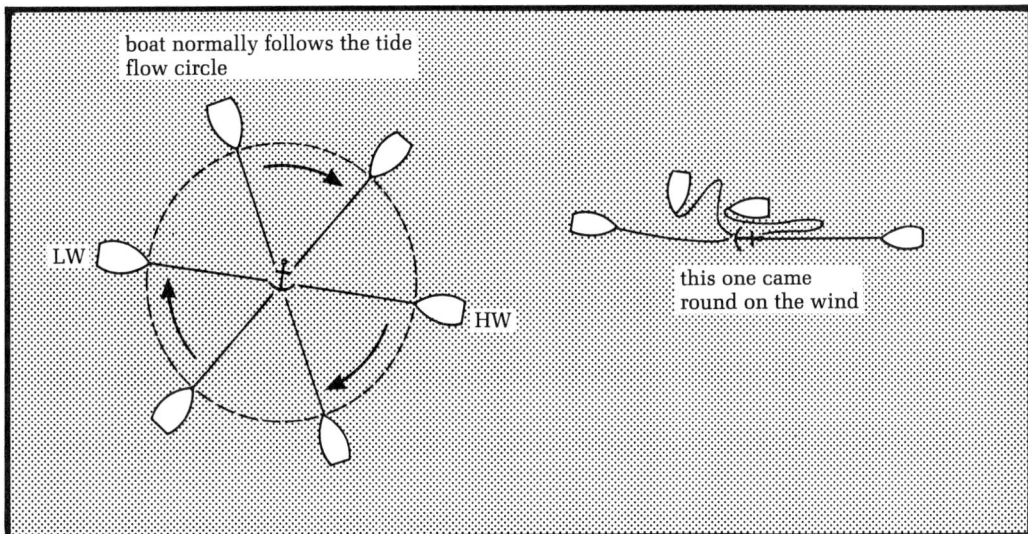

There are various ways for a boat to go around her anchor.

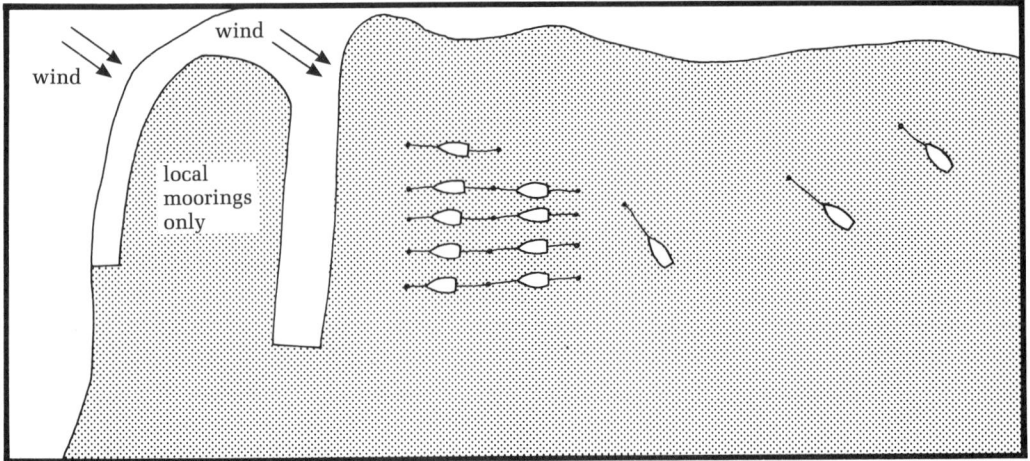

Typical anchorage. Where will you go?

one of the small, LCD screen video echo-sounders. This will give an actual picture of how the rocks are aligned and where the biggest patches of sand are located.

Where to Drop

The decision about where to let the anchor go is affected by a number of future factors.

Our little LCD video sounder is a valued anchorage tool.

Where will the boat actually be when she drops back on a prudent length of warp, not only for the present conditions, but for those that are expected? Amongst the considerations here are the changes in water depth as the tide ebbs and flows, the strength of the tidal current, especially if it is aggravated by a river, with another possibility that wind and tide might be in different directions. So where will her bows point?

The expected weather to come is also important. The boat might be lying with her nose towards the beach now, but where will she be if the wind goes on a reciprocal? Will she be safe if you are then on a lee shore? You must also consider the other boats in the anchorage and how much sea room to put between you and them. Generally speaking, boats swing to the anchor in concert, i.e. they go around their own circles and maintain their safe distance. Unfortunately, there are times when the usual does not happen: when one boat lies deep keel to the tide and another rides to the wind.

The prudent skipper also has safety in his mind. Yes, he is looking for convenience, but he is also looking to possible problems that might occur, not only if he drags his own anchor, but also if one of the other boats breaks loose. So, if you see a boat prowling around the anchorage, do not write him off as a ditherer, he might be the wisest skipper in the place.

The best places to anchor are very likely

It blew a gale at Muros . . .

to be taken up by local boat moorings and they will have been chosen for the winds experienced most often and most strongly. In normal, prevailing conditions, you should first hope to get amongst them, without risking fouling their moorings, or at least put yourself safely close to them. Equally, the weather at the moment might not be the usual wind direction, which might make another part of the harbour safer and better.

Our prudent, prowling skipper will be balancing all of these things in his mind as he motors around. He might be looking at the other boats and deciding that they are on light tackle and a 'piece of string'. It happens very frequently. These are neighbours to be avoided. You might even see him make a trip across to the other side of the bay, or into an adjacent cove. There he is looking at holding ground, hazards and water depth in case he should be forced to move there in the dark.

This recently happened to us at Muros, where we were anchored conveniently and interestingly close to the town quay and stayed there all through a gale-wracked Sunday, during which several boats broke out from their holding. By the end of the evening meal, we had suffered enough banging about, so we motored a short distance across the ria to get beneath the shelter of the mountains. It was like shifting from a maelstrom to a mill pond, where we drank our coffee in total sunlit peace and enjoyed a completely quiet,

. . . a mile away, St Anton was as calm as a mill pond.

moonlit night in 4m (13ft) of clear water, just below a village awakened by a crowing cock, a gently calling dog, fishermen rowing out to their nets and the smell of wood fires.

We spent a week commuting over to the town by dinghy and by shifting the parent boat, but returning to the fishing and the flat, clear calm of St Anton each evening.

Anchoring is not for the lazy.

Flaking for Ease

This dictum is borne out by watching how many people anchor the boat and then have to re-anchor, because the chain did not run and set properly, or because they got it caught in something on deck, or because a couple of twisted links jammed in the hawse-pipe.

The solution is to 'flake' the chain out on deck before you let the anchor go. It is laid up and down in the clear, so that it can have unimpeded progress outboard, free of all obstructions, including the feet of any crew involved. Using this method, you can inspect the links as you lay it out and even have two separate sections – one to equal the length of chain that you expect to set and the other as the spare and emergency, in case you have to let go of a bit extra.

Let her go

This 'anchoring is not for the lazy' philo-

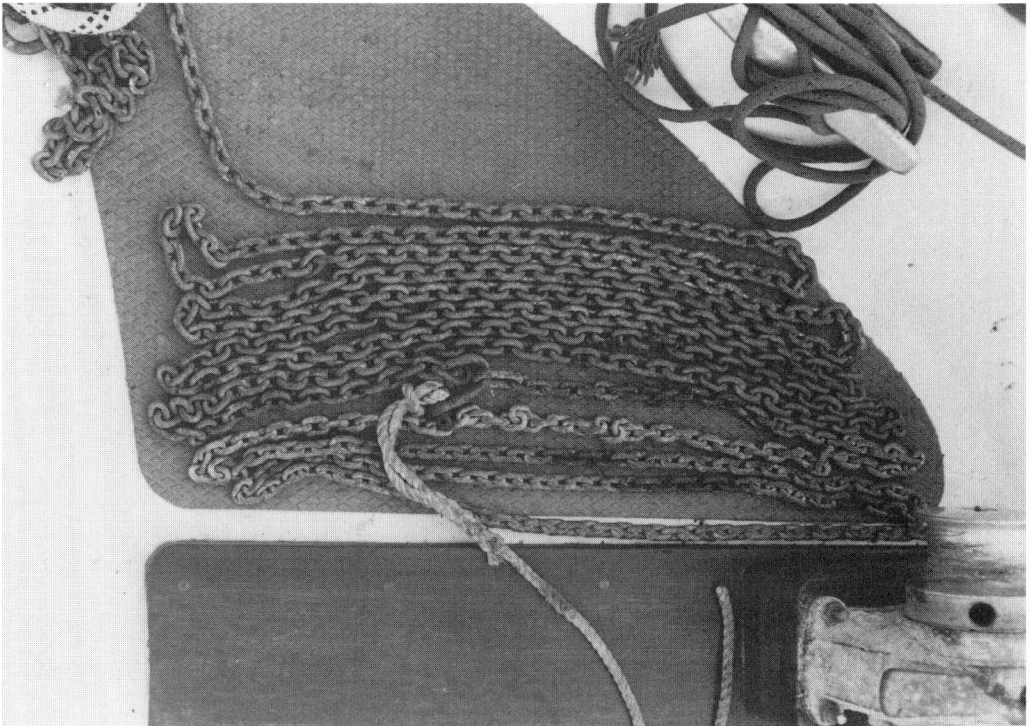

We always flake the chain out on the deck.

sophy applies even to the physical act of actually dropping the anchor onto the spot that you have chosen for best holding and to allow the boat to drop back on the wind and the tide to where you want her to be.

Automatic, power-driven anchoring systems, often remotely controlled from the wheel-house, are a mixed blessing here. They ignore the fundamental that a good skipper does a fair amount by feel.

The most efficient method is to let all the way come off the boat directly into the wind or tide. Whoever is on the helm might have to work a bit here to maintain a good heading. When there are no more ripples under the forefoot and she is dead stopped, let the anchor go and feel the chain run out over the bow roller and also lightly through your gloved hand. You will already have a good idea of depth from the echo-sounder and will also be able to feel when the metal hits the floor and the chain is 'up and down'.

Mark the Chain

Some anchor hardware incorporates a measuring device that counts the metres as you let them go. They are, however, prone to slip and are often not installed where they can easily be read, so most skippers fall back on old-fashioned, physical marking of the actual chain.

A simple system, easy to remember, is red, white and blue. A couple of links painted red at the 10m (33ft) point, then white and blue at 20 and 30m (66 and 98ft) are easy to identify. If you have more than this available, the next symbol is two bands of colour for each ensuing 10m

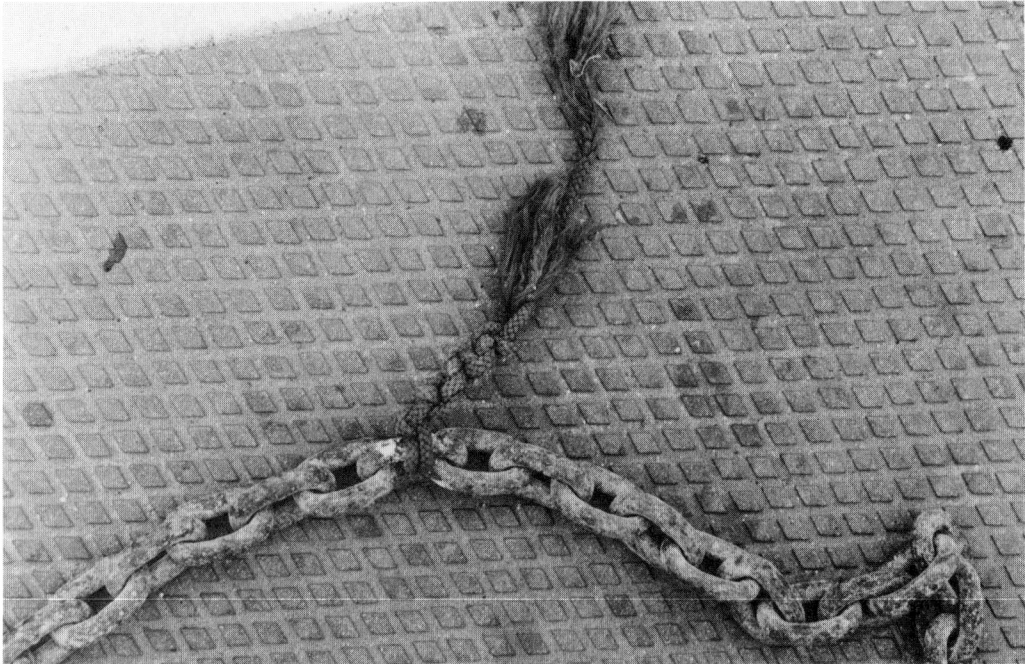

We mark our chain with coloured cord and paint.

We take a turn on the capstan and also tie off to a cleat.

(33ft). (The markings are also useful when you haul the anchor and are wondering just how much more there is to come in, or when the chain will be up and down and must be braced for breaking the anchor out of the ground.)

On the Bottom

At that point when you feel the anchor touch the sea-bed, you give the agreed signal for the helmsman to go astern in the straightest possible downwind/tide line – not nearly as easy as it sounds. As the boat drops back, you watch and count the number of metres/yards going out. When she gets off line, signal to put the engine in neutral, take a turn of chain around the windlass, or a cleat, and just hold on until the natural forces bring boat, chain and anchor back into their straight line.

You then repeat this process until you have let go of your desired scope of warp. What you are really doing here is not dropping anchor, but laying it. The essential is to keep some straight line way on the boat so that you get your chain in a nice, stretched line along the sea-bed. The danger is to let a whole pile of chain go with such a rattle that it piles up on top of itself and even atop the anchor. Then when the wind blows, it all comes out badly, the anchor is not dug in and may even be tripped out by its own chain.

Anchoring is not for the impatient, so the skipper bides his time. When he is satisfied, he makes the signal to go very firmly astern, not only to check that the chain is stretched, but also so that the boat pulls the anchor well in. By doing this, he has probably applied a force equal to, or greater than, any gust likely to come. It pays to be a bit brutal here.

When the engine is cut, the weight, or elasticity, of the warp usually pulls the boat forwards again. So the skipper stays in the bow to watch and to tie off the anchor to its strongest holding point. We use several turns around the capstan (never trust the gypsy alone) plus a safety end made fast to a cleat.

Final Touches

It is a good feeling when she is all snug and you can walk back to the cockpit. There, you locate and line up some shore marks, taken from the place where you would normally view them. The thinner (telegraph poles are ideal) you can make the closest one the better. The edge of a building makes a good near mark – or a far one. 'The street lamp on the middle window of the house with green shutters' is perfect. It is better still if it is immediately abeam, with similar good marks directly opposite on the other side of the boat and another astern.

Some skippers write these in the log, or sketch them on a piece of paper. On our own boat, I generally also take a couple of compass bearings, add a precise GPS position and a selection of radar bearings and distances to such precise places as harbour walls and fixed navigation marks. These all go in the log, together with a note of the time, the water depth, the wind, any current and the compass direction of the ship's head.

This is not being too fussy. Cruising should be fun and I enjoy doing these things, which are very useful information on a number of occasions. Only when we are totally confident and satisfied do we recheck the tie-off, put the batteries onto the domestic bank, shut down all the

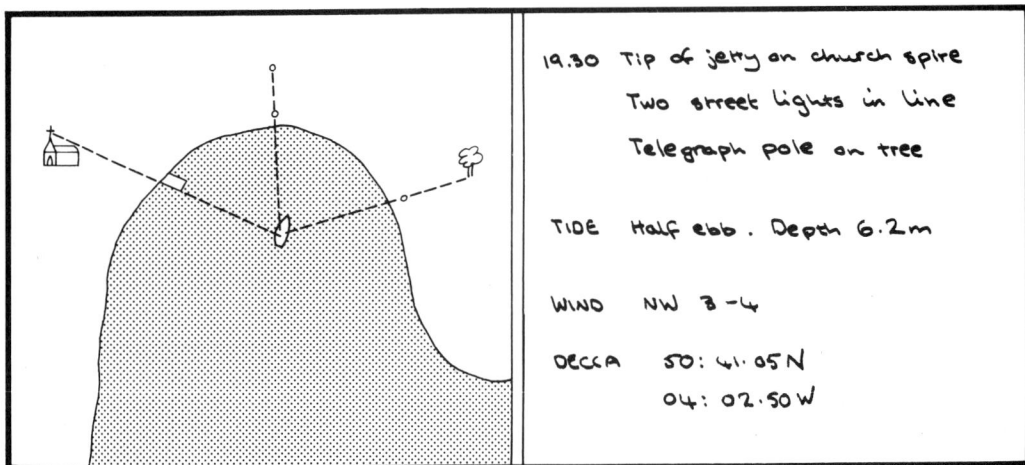

Sketch and write your shore marks on a piece of paper – or even put them in the log.

instruments, turn down the stern gland grease head, check the fuel, have a quick look around the engine compartment for leaks, wires jumping out of clips, etc., then play hunt the corkscrew.

Calculating the Scope

There is no real formula for deciding just how much anchor warp (scope) to let the boat have. This is dictated by the conditions, the maximum expected depth of water and how long you plan to stay. On a quiet day, when you stop for lunch, you can ride quite safely to twice the water depth. The traditional scope has generally been three times the water depth, which gives the chain a shallow enough angle to pull the anchor along the sea-bed, rather than up towards the surface. In a real blow, it pays to have out as much chain as you possess, not only for the trigonometrical reason above, but also to have the extra safety of maximum weight. In really bad weather, five or six times the water depth will certainly do no harm.

The Trip Line

A trip line is a long length of adequate cord, attached to the main body of the anchor and running up to a buoy. Its purpose is to offer a secondary directional pull to drag out an anchor that is caught under a ledge or tangled in a mooring chain. For this reason, the trip line must

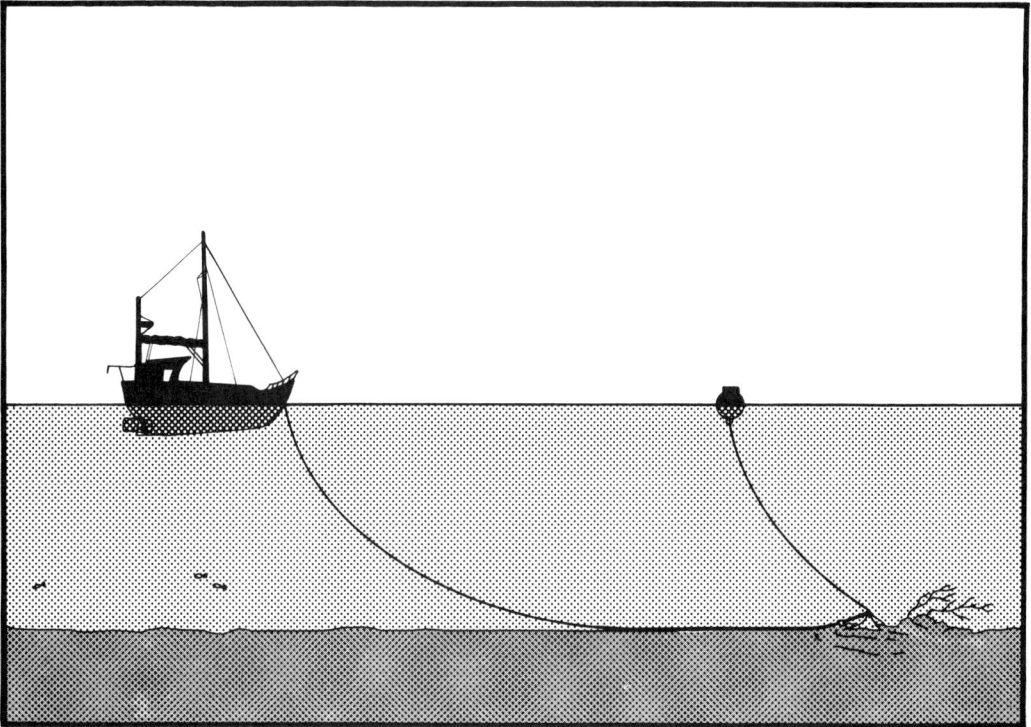

The trip line.

be strong enough to withstand the pull, which might be from the parent boat backed up-tide, or it might be from the dinghy whilst a crew member works the main engine to take all of the strain off the chain.

The trip line is not a completely certain device, so there might be occasions when you need another way of freeing yourself. (Nothing betters having your own, tame diver in the crew.) We, for instance, recently dragged across a hawser stretched at right angles along the sea floor. The capstan managed to haul the anchor and the steel wire up to about 3m (10ft) from the surface, where we could see the problem. We tried the old trick of a sudden release with a simultaneous hard astern, hoping that the anchor's weight would let it fall free. On this occasion it failed, so we hauled it taut again and sent a swimmer on a free dive to loop a rope under the obstruction. When this was made fast, we were able to lower the CQR to freedom and to go to sea with all our gear still intact.

Cleverer people have managed to drop a weighted line up-stream of the hazard and to retrieve the other end beneath the cable with a boat hook as it came down on the current. One cruising acquaintance keeps a couple of home-made, lightweight metal grapnel hooks, specifically for this relatively common occurrence. When he has retrieved his bower anchor, he abandons the grapnel hook by cutting its line off at the water-line.

Extra Holding Tips

A lightweight anchor and rope combination can be given increased holding power by hanging a heavy weight at a convenient distance down the warp. This can either be tied off, or allowed to slide down with a thin recovery line retained on board as a brake and adjuster. A length of hanked-up chain, or some rocks in a canvas bucket make a good weight. What you are seeking here is anything that will flatten the angle, or increase the horizontal component of pulling force.

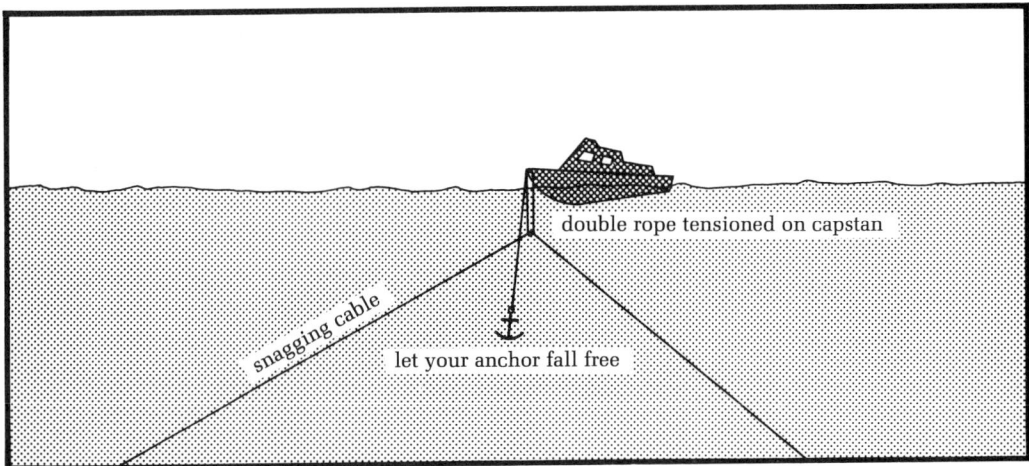

Hold the offending cable taut until you can let your anchor fall free beneath.

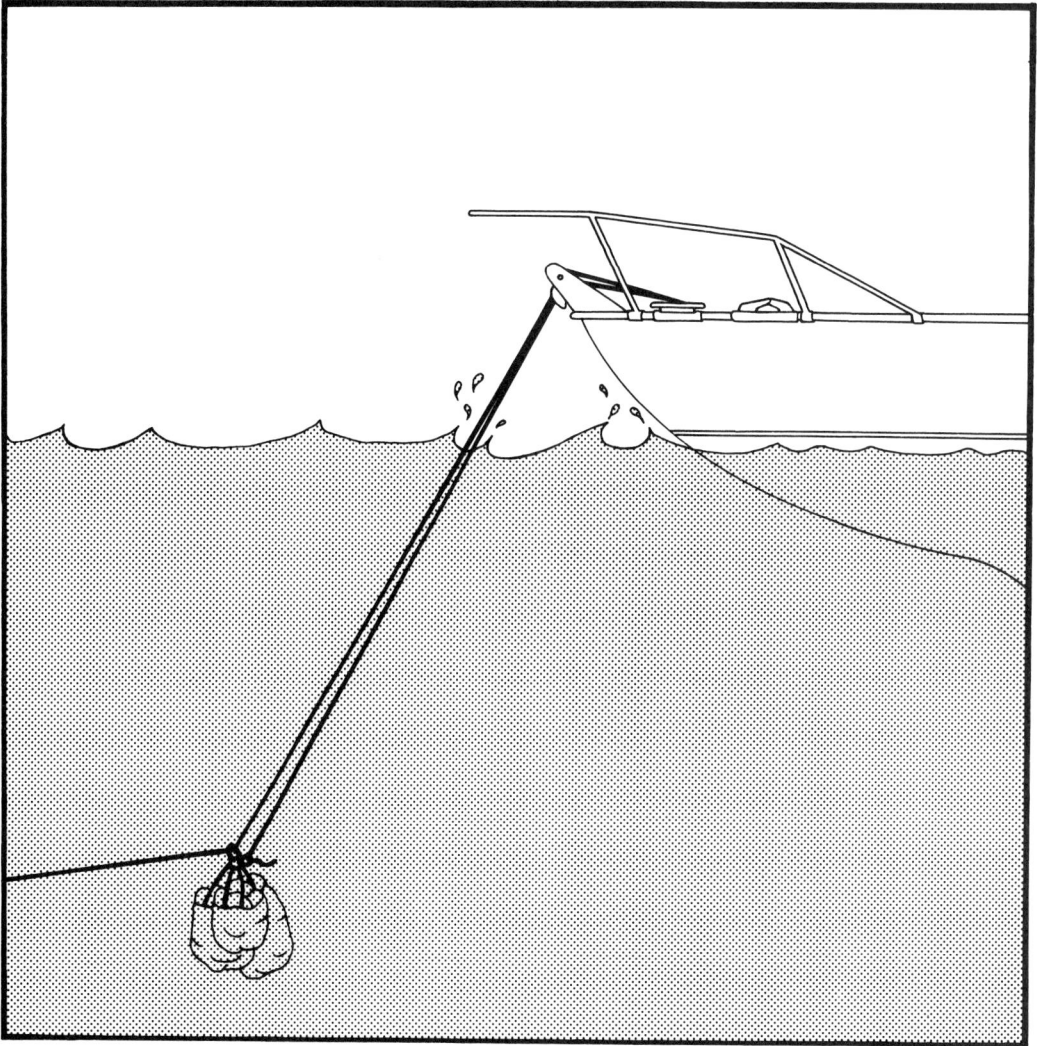

A heavy weight flattens the angle of pull.

The Kedge

In severe conditions, it becomes prudent to lay two (sometimes three) anchors by kedging the smaller, or an equal, to your main anchor – sometimes called the bower. The length of chain between the two is a matter of choice. We have a 5m (16ft) length of 10mm (0.4in) chain, which is shackled to the CQR's special kedge eye. It could also be wound round and shackled back to itself.

The purpose of the kedge is not only to increase the weight and to double the number of bites on the sea-bed, but also to hold the main anchor down. In most

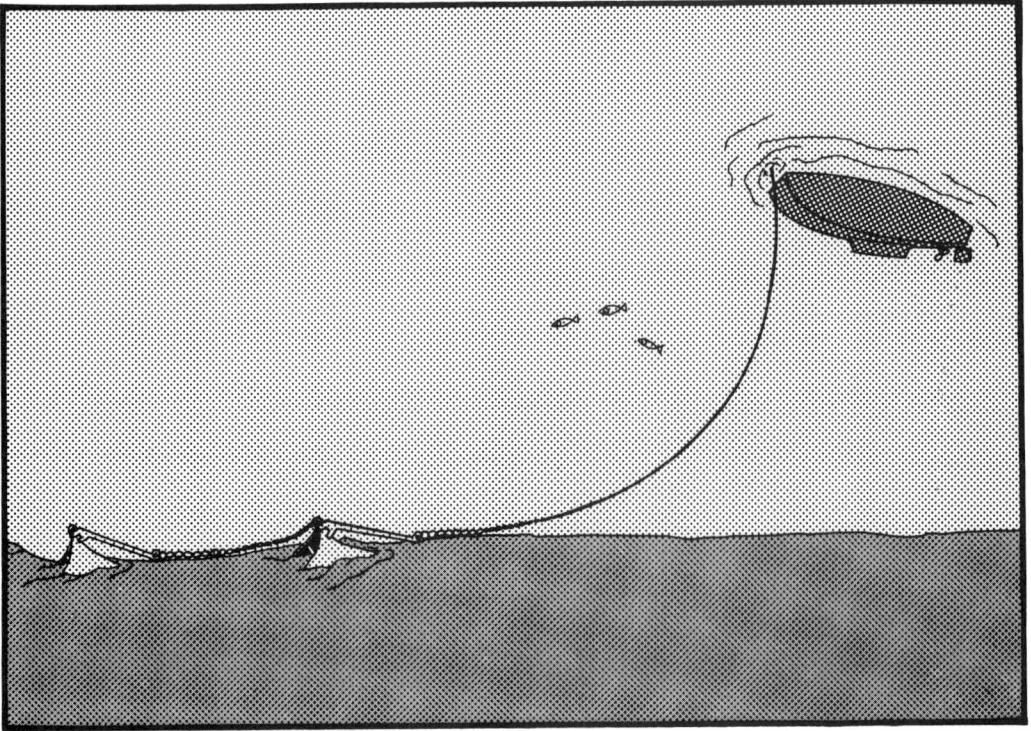

In some instances, only a kedged (double) anchor will hold.

circumstances it will retain its hold as the boat is circled around the bower, which might trip and reset.

It is always prudent to put a trip line on your kedge, because this makes it easier when you are retrieving both anchors simultaneously. The trip-line buoy might be at a fair distance from your own boat, so use something that makes it very obvious that it is not a mooring buoy. The last thing you want in a blow is for some lazy crew to come in at night and tie off to your kedge.

The Second Bower

Only *in extremis* will you need to lay a second main anchor. Getting it down is not *per se* a difficult operation. The problems are usually created by the wind and wave conditions which necessitate the extra precaution anyway. It also takes nearly as much labour to describe as to execute.

As always, riding to two anchors begins by deciding where you want the boat to lie. From that position, you motor forwards and off to port, in order to drop the first hook. At that point, get a good shore mark that will serve to locate the second dropping point, which should be the same distance up-tide as the first and about 15–20m (49–66ft) to the side.

When the boat has dropped back about twice the off-set distance, she is motored up to point two and the second hook is let

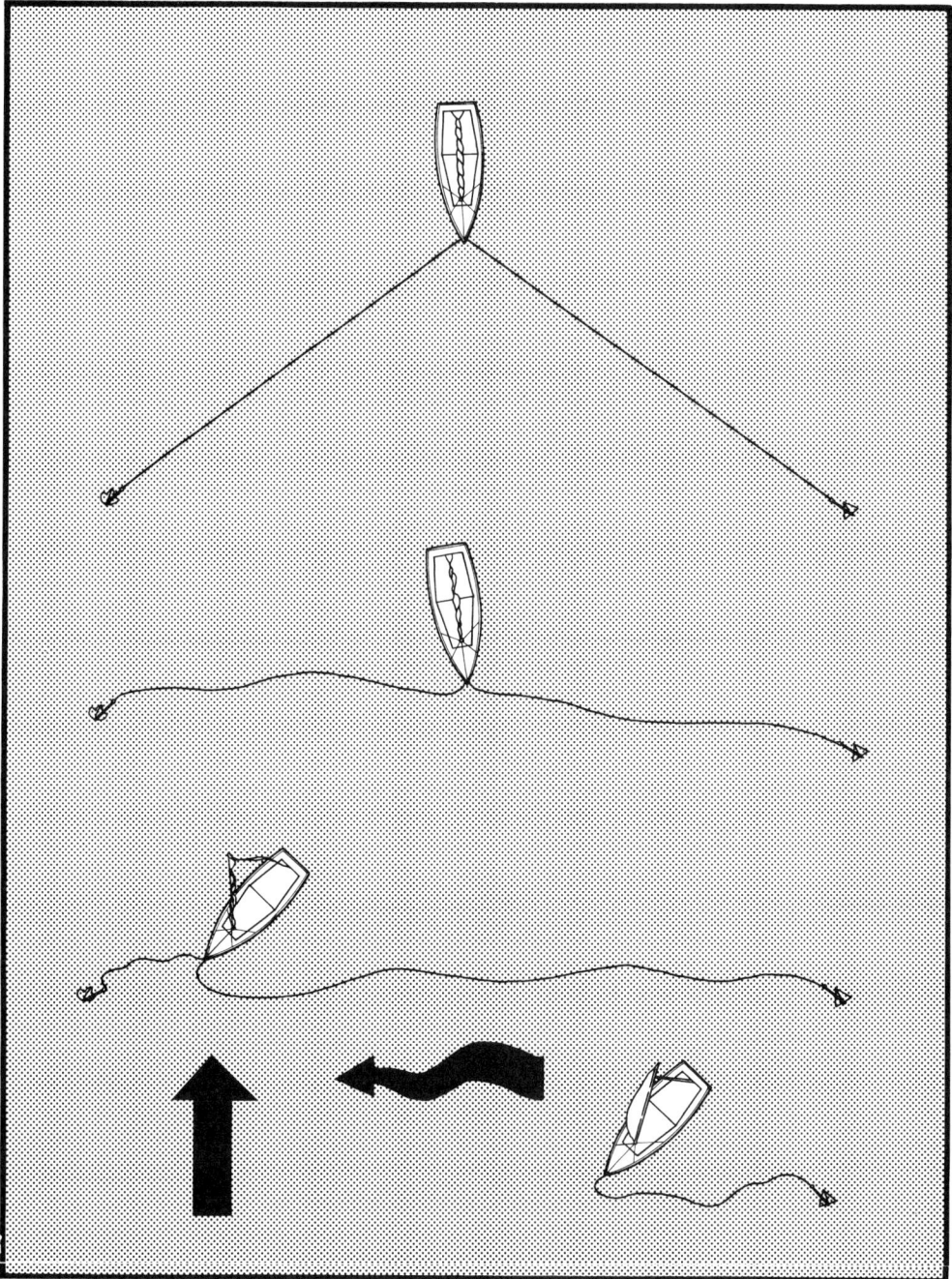

Settling to two anchors ready for a blow.

go. From here on, laying out the warp for a pair of anchors follows the same rules as for a single unit. Keep some stern way on the boat. Have patience. Firm up from time to time, with each anchor taking 50 per cent of the strain.

The final act is to settle the boat centrally between the pair, so that they are sharing the load equally. As the wave lifts the boat, both warps must come taut together – unless you see your reserve anchor simply as a safety precaution.

You may have to adjust the warp lengths every hour or so and will certainly need to take the twists out of the dual chain. These wrap around each other as the boat goes around its axis. Take them out when the weather permits as two turns are easier than a dozen caught up in the bow roller.

The Alternatives

There are different philosophies about taking the second anchor out in the dinghy. Some skippers swear by having all of the chain in the smaller boat, with the end already tied off to length aboard the parent boat. We prefer to have a reliable crew member feeding the chain off the yacht, whilst the other concentrates on steering the dinghy. Whichever method you use, coping with the weight of chain that will be out is always a battle – which is another reason for having your reserve anchor on a chain and rope combination.

The most ingenious way of putting out a second anchor was demonstrated to us by a very resourceful crew, on one of those days when there really was too much wind for a rowing dinghy to be safe. The anchor was tied off with a quick-release knot to a couple of fenders buoyant enough to support its weight. Two lads then donned swimming masks and fins in order to push the ensemble out to the appropriate position and to let it go as instructed.

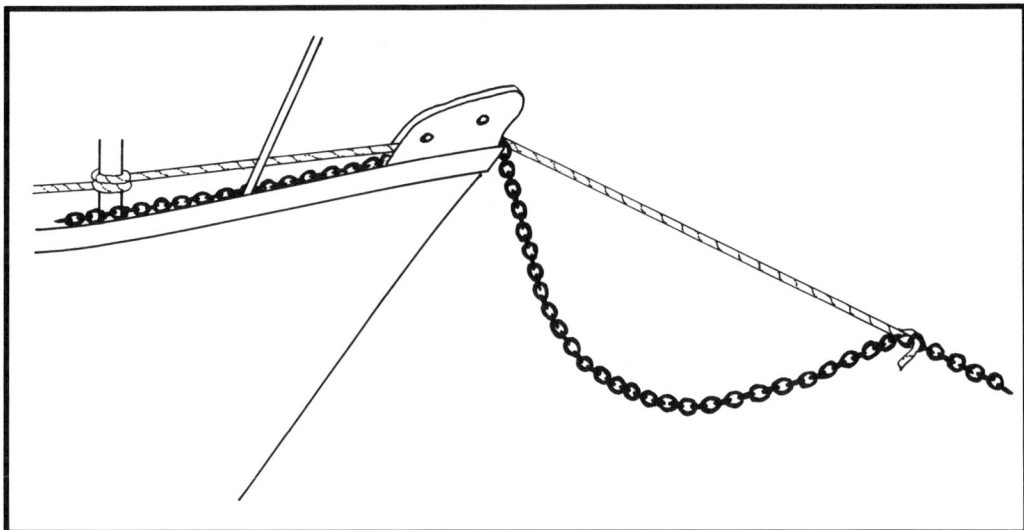

Using a rope snubber to stop chain rumbling.

The Bitter End

The very last inboard link of an anchor chain is called 'the bitter end' and the name has given rise to all those sayings about having reached it. The bitter end should always be made securely fast. When you are flaking on deck, you tie off closer to the anchor and make the free end fast as soon as it is out of the hawse-pipe.

In untangling twists, use a safety rope, i.e. find a tie-off, but the bitter end remains firmly tied 100 per cent of its time without fail. This is not being over-fussy. A heavy chain can disappear over the side at a frightening rate and can do a lot of human and marine damage in the process. If there is one situation I wish to avoid, it is falling on the deck, losing the anchor and being on a lee shore in a blow.

If you doubt that it happens, we recently watched a Dutch motor yacht attempt to anchor close to us in flat, foggy conditions. A crewman was sent forwards to do the work as the boat was eased astern. He completely let go of a large anchor and 100m (328ft) of chain – bitter end and all. It cost the owner about £200 for a diver to recover the gear, but even this was only 25 per cent of the replacement costs.

SUMMARY

- Do not let anchoring become a lost art. It could well save your life.

- Criteria for choice: the anchor must suit the boat and the holding ground.

- Belt and braces pays in weight and warp.

- All warps must have some 'give' in them.

- Do not let the chain pile up on the floor. Use the boat to lay it along the sea-bed.

- Watch how the other boats are aligned prior to selecting your drop spot.

- Flake the anchor chain out on the deck both for easy dropping and safety.

- The simplicity of red, white and blue chain scope markings.

- Your hand signals from bow to helm will be essential, personal and automatic.

- Don't be lazy. When the wind blows hard, up-anchor, go looking for a lee.

5

BERTHING

All human pursuits have their own methods of making a very rapid assessment of a person's competence. With equestrianism, it is watching the way the rider mounts from the floor. In boats, you ask the sailor to pick up a mooring buoy, or to put the vessel alongside. The incompetent will either refuse, or foul it up. The competent will smile a message that says, 'OK, it's your boat' and will just get on with it.

The Spanish pilot who took our 9m (30ft) motor sailer into the dangerous Ria de Ortiguera popped her safely alongside the quay wall with ease and was able to step ashore even before we had made fast the warps. Later that afternoon, he performed the same magic with a 6,000-tonne (5,904-ton) German freighter.

These very good boat handlers have a natural feel, which allows them to berth anything from cargo boats to dinghies. Tragically, there are others who never seem to get it right. It may well be that the only real differences between these two poles are those of planning and observation.

The expert has a clearly formulated plan of every part of his manoeuvre, including contingencies for mishaps. He also has everything on deck, ready and in place, well before the berth is reached. All of

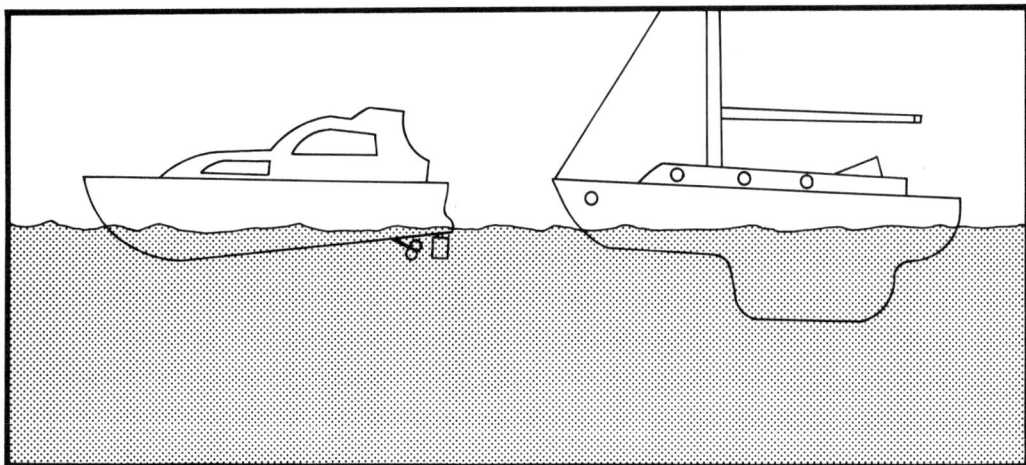

Problem. Motor cruisers will probably be wind rode, but the deep-keeled sail boats will be into the tide.

these decisions are reached in the light of his observations of prevailing conditions, and he never takes his eye off the boat's behaviour during the operation. He is always using what is available, and he never makes any sudden changes of direction. Everything is done with confidence, but slowly enough to have the boat always under control.

In contrast, our non-expert will charge up between the marina pontoons, with ropes and fenders still in lockers and no boat hook in sight. He has no real plan of where he intends to go, nor on which side his berth will be. At the last minute, he spots a gap and attempts a brusque, right-angled swing in across the wind and tide and then wonders why he is suddenly diagonally across the slot.

The berthing moral must be to stop, think, choose, observe wind and tide, notice what the other boats are doing, pick the widest possible arc to target, tell everybody on board what you plan to do, then execute the programme slowly.

Picking up a Buoy

This philosophy should apply even to the very basic boat-handling task of picking up a mooring buoy in an uncrowded anchorage. Yet many crews stiffen with fright about this and have bad dreams about missing the buoy with the boat hook, falling overboard, or getting the line around the propeller. The problems are (1) positioning the boat, (2) grabbing the buoy and (3) holding the boat whilst a rope is made fast.

Your best indicator of how to put the boat 'on the glide path' will be from observation of other craft already at rest. If there are none, any skipper worth his salt will

have had a look at the wind indicator, or noticed if there is actually any current tugging at the buoy itself.

The line of approach must be into whichever is the stronger force, not only to stop the boat, but also because this is how she will eventually lie to the mooring. There is also the logic that you cannot really control a boat going down-tide, or downwind, unless you are travelling faster than the propelling medium. Speed is the last thing you want here.

There are skippers who argue that they will have a buoy picked up only in the very eyes of the ship, because that is where you make it fast, so it is best to be as close as possible. It is when you see crew members stretched out flat in trepidation, with a boat hook waving about at arm's length and repeatedly missing the eye, that you begin to think that there must be a better way. If you are crewed by a squad of gorillas who can just brute force the buoy aboard, some problems are solved, but even they have difficulties right up on the bow – which is generally the highest part of the boat and is certainly the part that goes up and down the most in waves.

Bow pickers also miss the buoy because the skipper loses sight of it under the bow flare, so he does not really know whether it has vanished to port or to starboard.

A Better Way

Short-handed crews (such as couples) simply have to find a different way of doing things. Our own involves discussing which side we want to pick up the buoy. Supposing it is to port. The first task is to attach a medium-weight line to a bow cleat and then to lead it out around the stays to a point almost amidships. At this location, we also prepare either one, or

The bow goes up and down more in the waves.

two heavy-duty mooring ropes, already un-hanked so that their coils will run free.

The boat is then steered up-tide, on a path about 5m (16ft) to starboard of the buoy, which would pass down the port side if allowed to continue and where the helmsman can see it. Just about when the buoy is reached, the boat is turned slightly, diagonally across the tide and slowed right down. This angle means that she then moves sideways, under control, in the canoeists' 'ferry glide' mode.

The aim is to pick up the moorings slightly forward of amidships when the boat is being pushed down onto the buoy, which is also sheltered in the lee of the hull if there are any waves. In fact, we do not initially attempt to pick it right up. The first task is to get the medium rope through the ring or the chain and to make the free end fast – even amidships if necessary. 'Get it made fast somewhere, so that we can hold the weight of the boat', is the prime consideration.

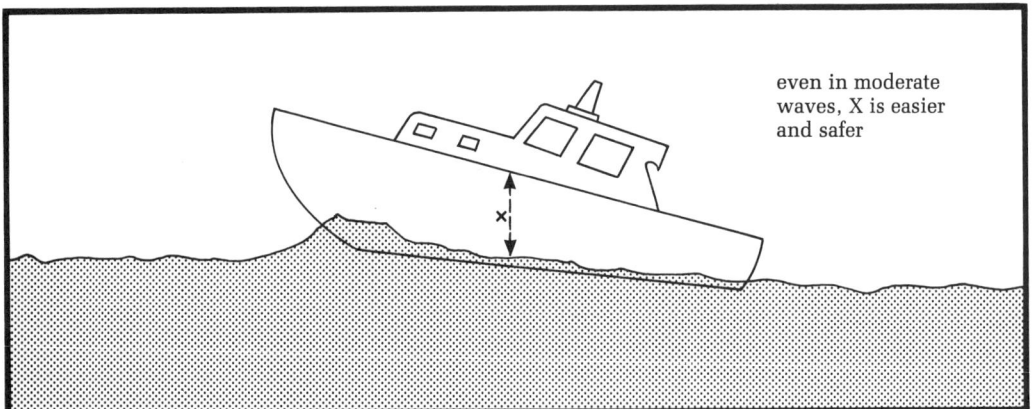

Pick up the buoy amidships where it is not so high.

This useful grabber hook comes attached to a pole and can be used to snag lines, the rings at the top of mooring buoys or the cleats on a dock.

Even in calm conditions it is safer and more convenient to pick up a mooring from an amidships position, especially on a high-sided boat like this trawler yacht.

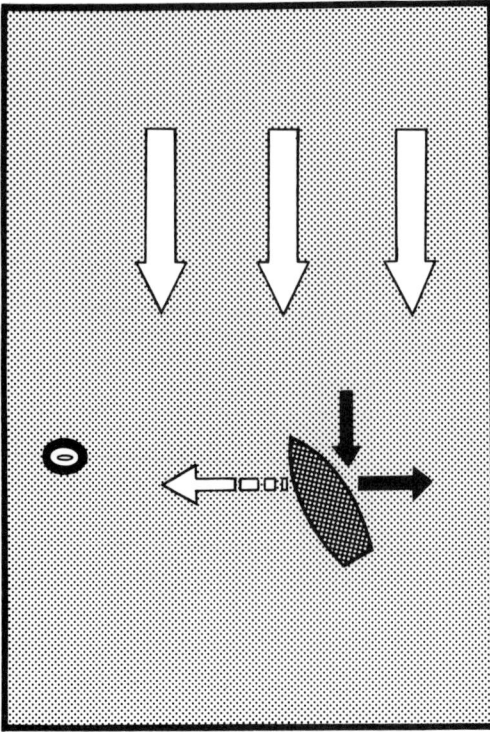

Let the elements ferry glide you across to the buoy.

With a heavy buoy in a big tide, it might rub your hull, but this is better than missing the mooring. In our case, as soon as I see that the medium line is on, I give the engine a kick astern to blast the buoy towards the bow, or I go ahead to starboard to fight the tide and to keep the buoy *in situ*. There are no firm rules.

Even though the main aim is to get a rope on somehow, on most occasions this works so well that we are able to take our time and even to put on a heavy line. By choice, we always take two turns of this around the ring to prevent rope chafe and on rougher occasions will put on two ropes by the same method and bring them in via bow fairlead on both sides.

Pride Comes Before

If the pick-up looks as though it is going to be very problematical, we even send the dinghy on ahead with the medium line and one crew member, whilst the other brings the parent ship alongside to take it. This can be useful in waves, and has been even more useful on our own moorings, where we have had a six-knot current pulling the marker buoy almost beneath the surface.

There is no way that we could hold 7.5 tonnes (7.4 tons) against that, so we get some sort of line on from the dinghy, then put a rolling hitch as far down the chain as I can reach. This rope is pulled in with the windlass and the engine going ahead. When it reaches deck height and has been tied off, a second rope is put down the chain and the operation repeated.

Under Sail

Picking up under sail is a duplicate of the proceedings above, but is more a matter of knowing how much your boat will carry her way when you turn her into the tide. This apart, the diagonal approach can still be copied, with the reservation that you cannot afford to bring the buoy quite as far aft for pick-up, because you have fewer positive escape possibilities.

Even if we pick up with sails set, we always have the engine running 'just in case'. Our boat and crew are both valuable parts of our lives, so we are prepared to swallow our pride by doing things the easy way. This reasoning has extended to having a big dahn buoy with a firm grab handle sticking 1.2m (4ft) above sea level. That is very easy to grab. Our present mooring has a huge main buoy with the chain looped beneath and a small pick-up buoy on about 1.8m (6ft) of rope. The boat hook easily locates this free fathom, and when we haul we are lifting only untensioned chain.

Coming Alongside

In simple docking situations, even in those where the parking space is a bit tight between other boats, the advice offered in Chapter 2 remains valid, especially in tandem with the planning and observation already counselled above.

In all berthing operations, the wind and the tide can be your best friends or your greatest enemies. You must know exactly what both will do to your boat. Put another way, you must either choose a berth into which they will help you, or discuss a plan to beat them.

The Classic Assists

The perfect example of using one of these agencies to help is probably appreciated when putting a high-windage boat alongside a marina pontoon finger. Many of these are so low that you lose sight of them under the flare of the bow. So you pray for a berth with a side wind, put her nicely into the middle of the berth space and let the wind blow you gently on.

The wind does not need to be directly abeam. In fact, diagonally ahead works just as well and even slows the boat. It also means that the wind will be from a direction giving better shelter in the cockpit, rather than blowing straight into the saloon.

If the wind does not co-operate, either because it is too gusty, or because it is coming from entirely the wrong direction for the only available berth, there is no harm in swallowing your pride by going alongside the boat on the other side of the slot. You can then take your own mooring lines across to your chosen, protruding pontoon (without being under pressure) and can warp the vessel across on the winches. In very blustery conditions, I would even go alongside one of the boats in front of and behind my small quayside gap (illustrated in Chapter 2), then ease her into that small space on a combination of shore lines and the engine. It is better to dent your ego than your boat.

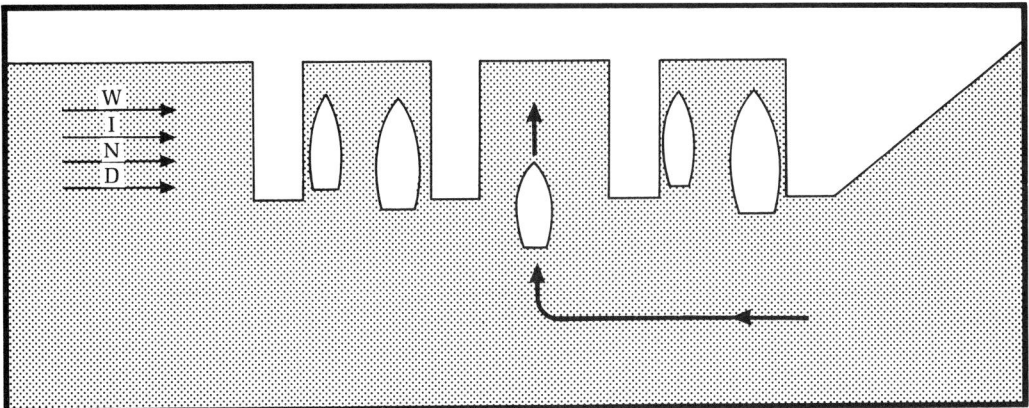

Aim for the middle and let the wind blow you gently in.

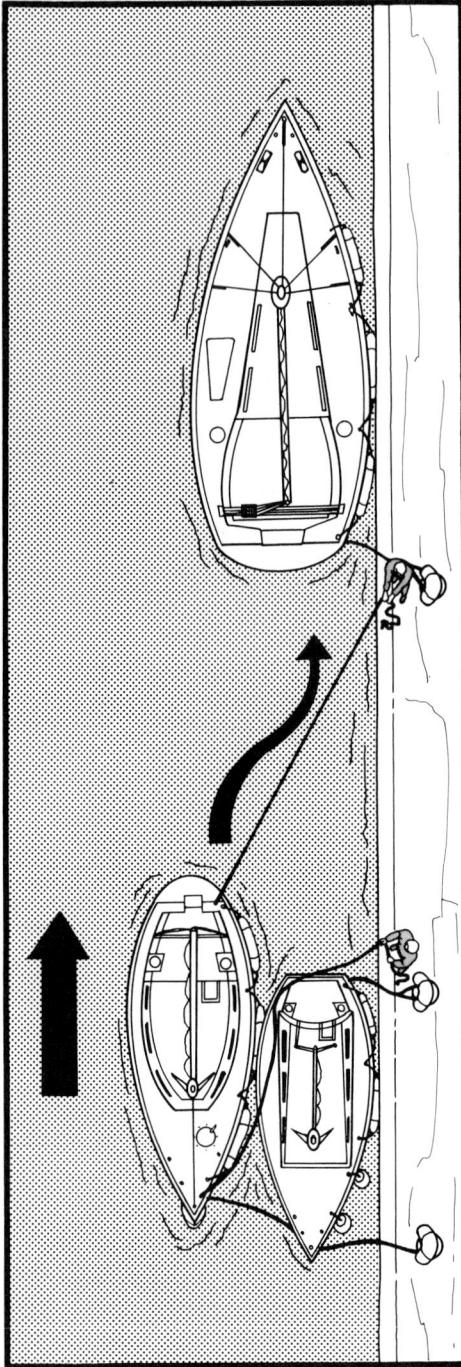

Go alongside the next boat, then warp yourself back to your chosen station.

If the gap is very small, it is easier to get in with a bit of head tide than in still water. The ferry glide really is a most useful seamanship skill to learn. Playing the engine revs will hold the boat nicely in the centre of the gap, whilst the tide gently eases her in sideways.

If you wish to see this wind/tide/sideways shift technique demonstrated *par excellence*, go to a big fishing port and admire the way in which skippers of huge, high-sided, single-screw trawlers drop them gently in sideways. This will also confirm the reason for my emphasis on not being in a hurry. Berthing sideways is a manoeuvre of slow, patient sense.

Using the Warps

There are also wind and tide situations in which firmer action is needed to get safely into the chosen space and even severe enough to force you into getting one warp ashore as a brake to be powered against by the engine.

The simplest of these is a warp made fast to a midships cleat. The free end is secured ashore, alongside the stern of the yacht. If the boat is powered gently ahead, she will be held firmly against her fenders whilst the rest of the ropes are put on more permanently.

Using warps as brakes and holders against wind and current is largely a matter of common sense, plus visualizing the effects of your actions. Any strain applied amidships will pull the boat bodily towards it.

Tension at the bows causes the fore end to swing in and the after end to move away from the wall. The more you pull the bow in at right angles to its cleat, the more pronounced the outward swing of the stern. The converse is also true.

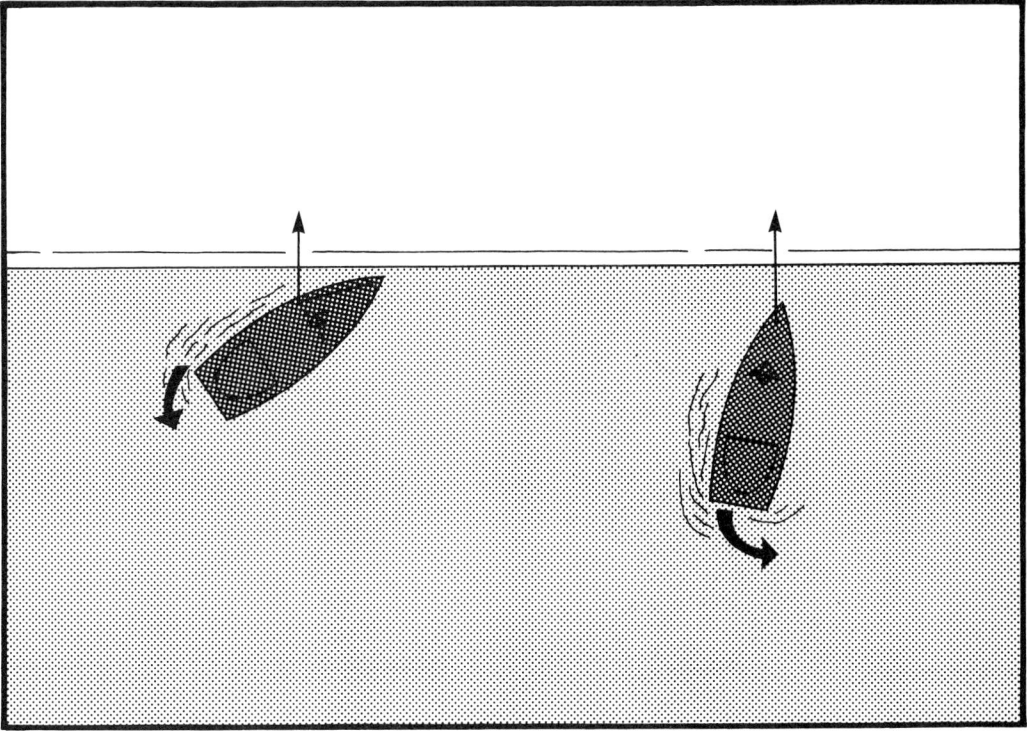

Problem: you pull the bow in and the stern swings out.

The Short-handed Brake

Once you have realized this fundamental, there are all sorts of ways to hold the boat safe and secure in a temporary position, whilst you get more permanent ropes into place.

If you are short-crewed (even single-handed) and have a free quay bollard just about anywhere along the boat's length, you can make a temporary mooring by putting a crewman ashore with two ropes – attached bow and stern. By taking a turn with both ropes around the bollard, but taking individual lines in, or letting them slide singly, the boat can be cajoled into position.

Once more the rules apply. If the bollard is close to the stern, the rear will be pinched in and the bow will swing out. The opposite also applies.

Warps and Springs

Once you have the boat more or less where you would like her to stay, the task is to make sure that she does not stray from there – to hit the boat behind, or even to move forward on the tide, either to a rough piece of wall, or to a place where there is no ladder.

The guiding principle is to have a long warp out in the direction of the prevailing wind or the current flow. As a rule of

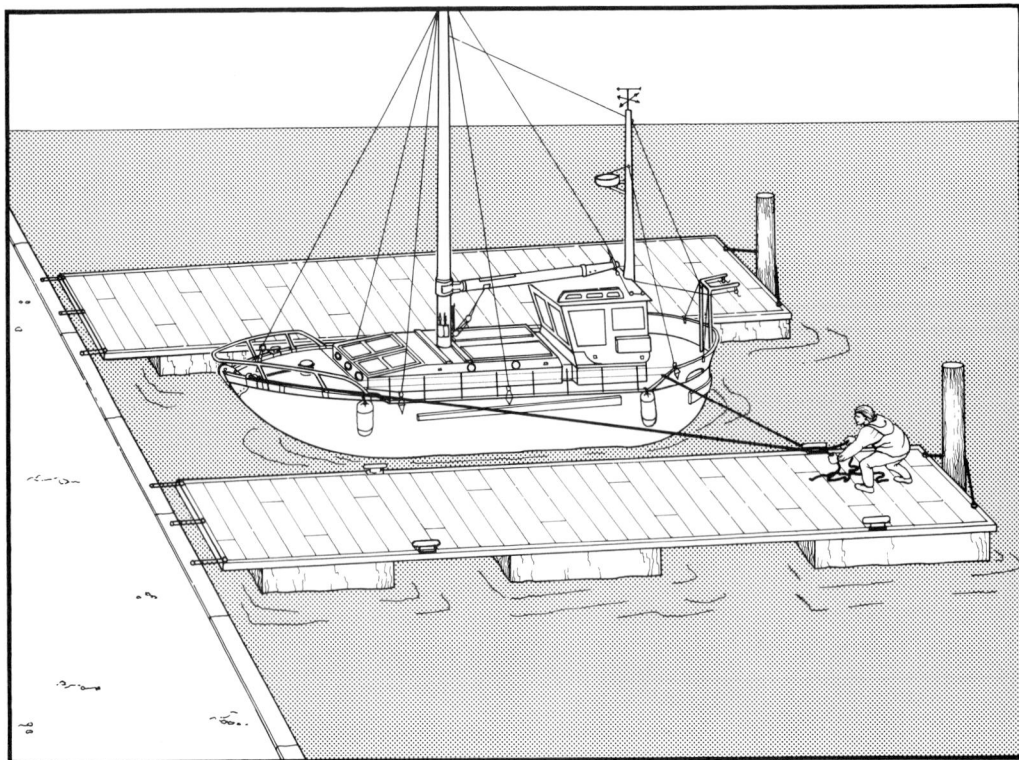

Put the crew ashore with two warps.

thumb, this should be at least three times the length of the predicted maximum tidal rise and fall. The boat will then drop back and will principally be held by that line. In this instance, imagine that the wind is on the bow, which means that the boat will move back as the tide rises and be pulled forwards again as it falls. The stern line must be slack enough to allow this, but must also be strong enough to cope if the wind or tide makes a 180-degree shift of direction.

These are the principal warps. Their assistants are a bow springer and a stern springer. The bow springer is led from the front of the boat to a ring close to the stern, or even beyond it. Its function is to hold the bow close to the wall, without pinching it in too tight and to inhibit forward motion. A stern springer is from a point aft, up to a tie-off near the bow. It holds the stern in close and stops the boat being driven backwards. Many yachts do not have a good solid cleat amidships, because it can detract from the 'flush deck' look preferred by many designers. If you have one, it can be very useful and, in the case of setting spring lines, means that they can be considerably shorter than the fore and aft version described above.

The final ropes are breast ropes out from bow and stern, made fast at right angles to their on-board cleats. They tension bow and stern against each other, so that neither crashes into the wall. They also hold both ends of the boat so that the crew can step ashore without fear of doing the splits.

Berthing alongside other Boats

Lying alongside other yachts, whether they are alongside a quay, between piles, or on a buoy, is only a slight variant on the six-rope array above. You want your own boat to be safe, but do not wish to upset the neighbours.

The main consideration is to think of the person who arrived first and who has probably taken the time and trouble to balance his own boat so that she lies nicely to her warps, with her fenders set where they best protect his hull from the wall, or from uneven pilings.

Then some clown comes alongside and just ties off to him fore and aft and might even put out totally meaningless springers. Suddenly his own boat is out of berthing balance. Gusts of wind swing her bow in so that unfendered portions hit the wall, and there are now two boats being held by ropes set for one.

Courtesy and care demand that you immediately put your own warps onto the shore and that you get them far enough ahead and astern so that they take their own strain at such an angle that you do not cause the inside boat to pinch its bows or stern into the wall, where they get damaged whilst you (the criminal) remain safe.

If he is on board, ask the skipper if your being being alongside would create any problems. He might be a fin keeler in a drying harbour and could fall outwards onto you. The boats might be of

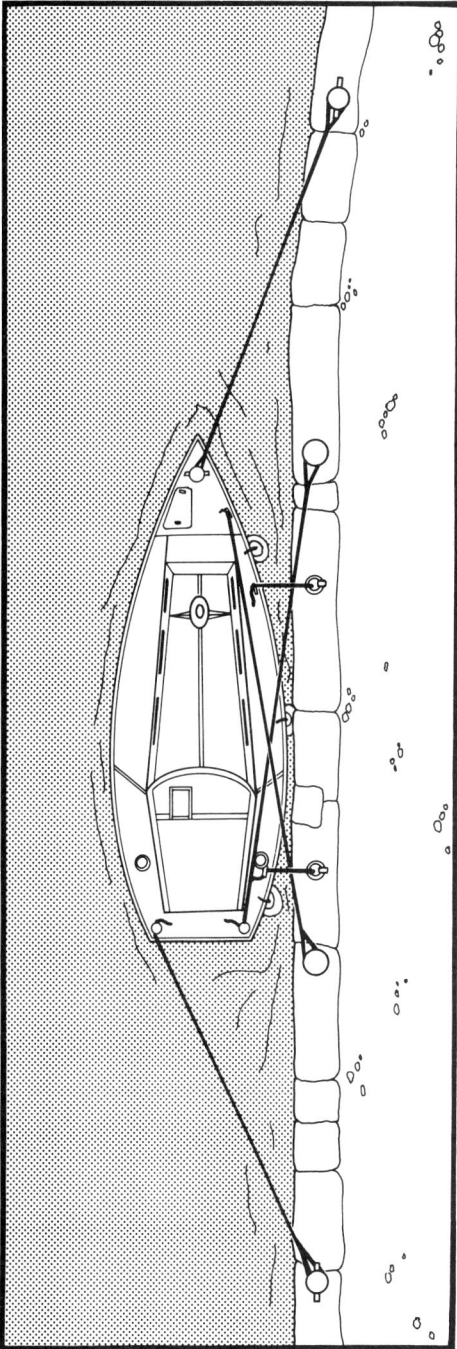

A standard six-warp mooring line arrangement.

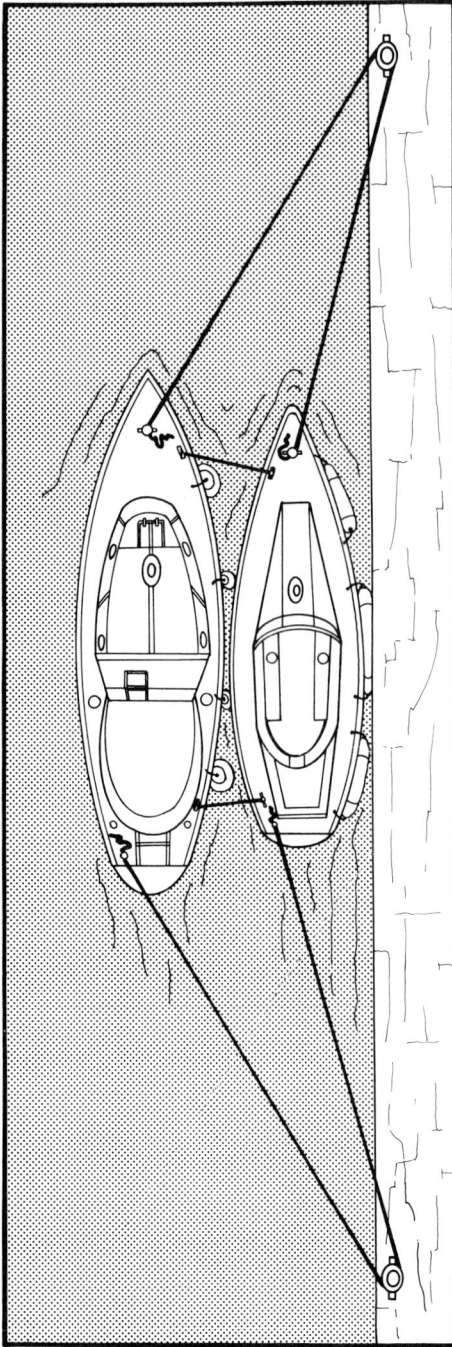

Neighbourly consideration demands properly placed warps so that you do not upset the balance of the other boat.

incompatible length or draught and would then make very uneasy bedfellows. Remember that the other person got there first and has done his work. Your arrival can only be to his disadvantage.

If he is amenable to your presence, at least acknowledge the favour. Always cross quietly in front of his mast to get ashore, and be polite enough to kick all sand, water and ladder weed off your shoes before you walk across his decks.

Much the same rules apply to buoys and piles. In addition to putting breast ropes onto the yacht that was there first, so that they keep the two square to each other, get a good, heavy rope onto the buoy and stay around long enough to see that it is taking the weight of your own boat, without unbalancing the other.

Taking the Ground Alongside

One often feels sorry for the skipper who will not let his boat go aground in harbour, even if 'will not' is replaced by 'cannot', because his boat is unsuitable and can only be left to dry out with difficulty. Some of our favourite berths are in small, drying harbours, where you are often left undisturbed by money-grabbing functionaries and the locals have time to give you information and advice.

Practically speaking, drying out is something of a mixed blessing. In its favour is the fact that when the boat is on the bottom, she is quite still for cooking and is not damaging her topsides by surging up and down a rough wall. On the contra side, few boats go down completely level and they often position themselves to make getting to a ladder a real feat of gymnastics.

Like all marine activities, doing it well means having the maximum amount of information. You need to know your boat and you need to know something about the drying quay and the nature of the sea-bed alongside.

The Suitable Boat

The best boats to put on the floor are those that are designed with drying out in mind. These are generally twin keelers, whose undersides have been specially strengthened to withstand the strain and the pounding that might occur. Consideration has also been given to the rudder. It is either strengthened and designed to be a robust, third point of balance, or it is kept well clear of the floor. Props are not a problem, except on some motor boats.

When we went looking for our own motor sailer, we deliberately sought a long keeler, on which the grounded weight is distributed along the whole length of the keel, with provision already in place for the addition of bilge plates.

A number of commercial and dual-purpose hulls already have strengthened flats for bilge keels built into the hull, in a combination of wood and heavy-duty glass-reinforced plastic (GRP) lay-up. The bottoms of the bilge keels are kept five centimetres (a couple of inches) above the level of the main keel, in order to obviate damage if she goes down on rough, stony ground. She can still roll clear. The boat

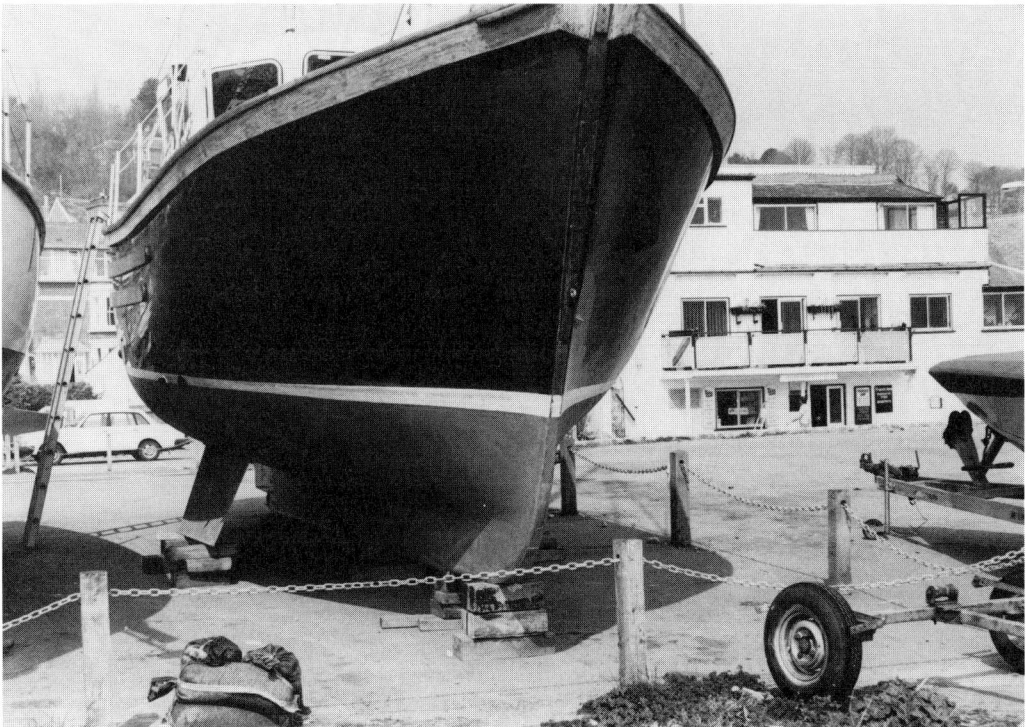

Bilge plates make her very safe when she is in winter storage.

71

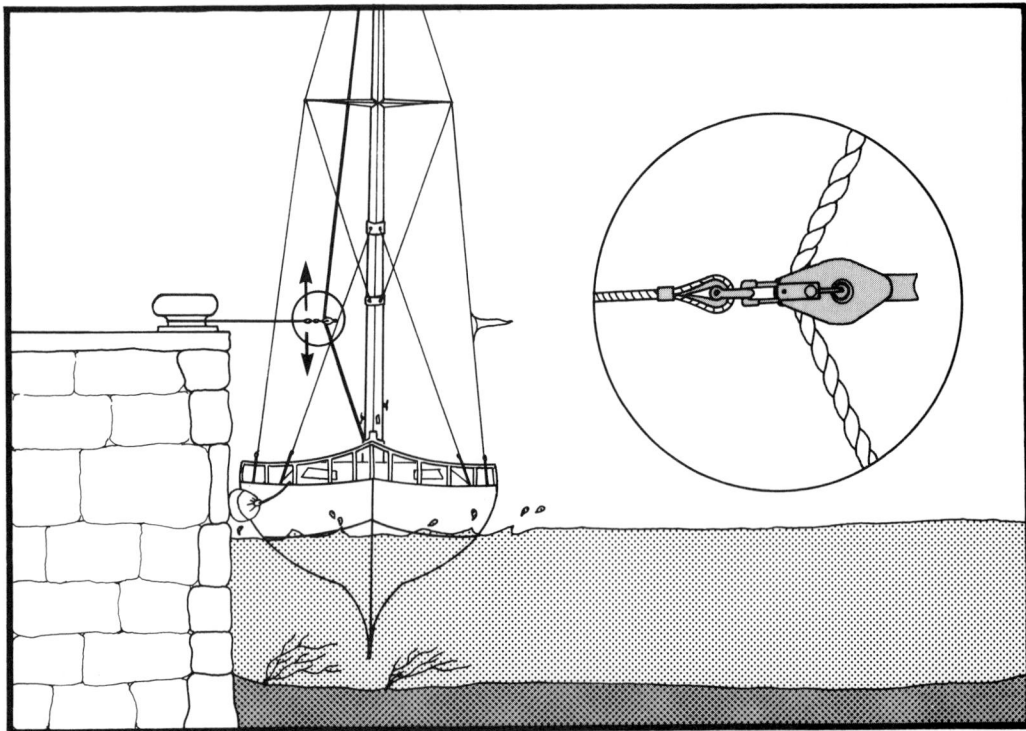

A fin keeler can be held upright with a block on a tautened halyard.

does not settle level, which is not too problematic apart from the fact that we can pour only half glasses of wine and the water will not run out of the shower tray.

A further advantage of the bilge keeler, or the twin keeler, is that you do not need to have a special cradle for the boat to sit on whilst she is on the hard standing during the winter.

Fin Keels Too

Fin keelers are more of a problem, but any moderately determined owner will manage. The problem is obviously that of ensuring that the boat settles completely in an upright position, or – better still – is supported on her own keel and leaning

very slightly into the wall. There are various ways of achieving this.

1 Put sufficient weight on the appropriate side to induce a visible list into the wall.
2 Take a masthead/mid-mast halyard ashore and tie it off to a strong point. The further away from the boat, the better, in order to increase the angle of pull at the top of the mast.

This rope might need constant attention to keep it taut as she goes down. Alternatively, hang a heavy weight one-third of its length out from the boat and let gravity and catenation do the work. In any event, put a flag on the rope to warn quay strollers that they risk decapitation.
3 Put a stout halyard through a pulley

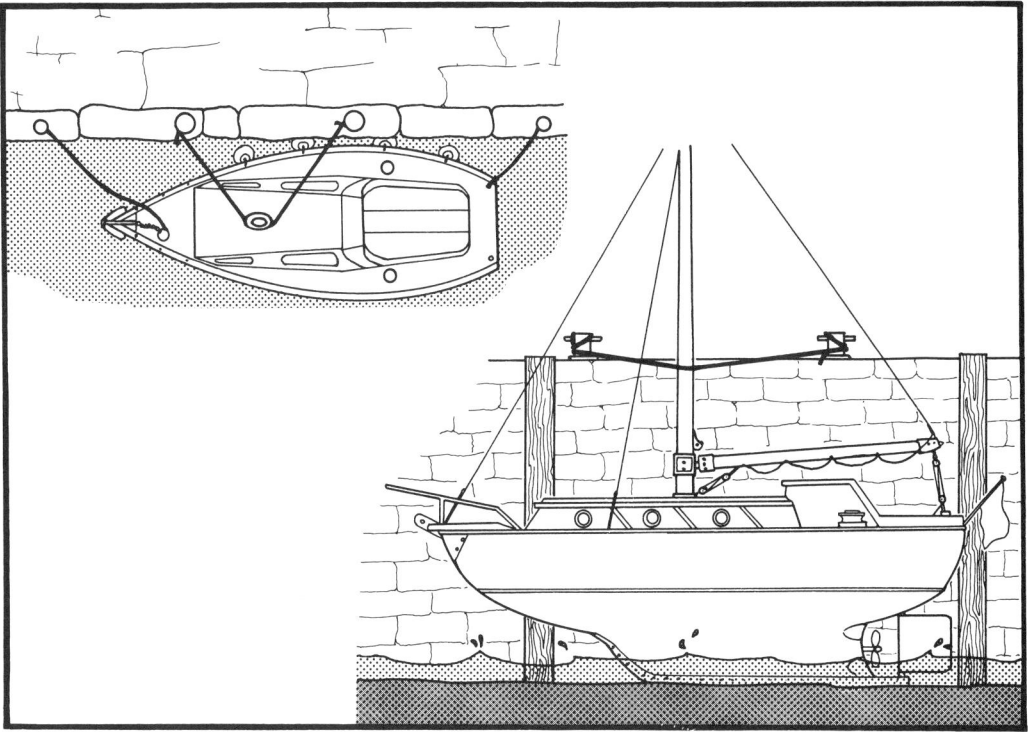

Loop a rope around the mast for added support.

block, and tension it hard in against the mast. The block is then attached to a shore point so that it holds the boat in, but finds its own height on the halyard. She will still need watching as she goes down, and a light boat will still need some weight on its shore side, just as soon as you first feel her touch the ground.

4   If your mast is free of obstructions, put a couple of loops of rope, fore and aft from the quay, around the mast. This longbow-shaped arrangement is very strong, very forgiving to the mast and very effective. If the quay is suitable, this method comes with the 'highly recommended' tag.

Know the Terrain

Cruising history is sprinkled with sad stories of boats being damaged by drying out against unsuitable walls and onto unsuitable floors. A personal acquaintance once let his boat go down onto a small barge that had sunk alongside. Fortunately, it was very calm and he was still aboard at the critical time, so the damage was cosmetic.

In this situation there is no substitute for local knowledge. The harbourmaster or the local sailing club are amongst the best consultants, plus there is no better method than a personal inspection, or watching what has happened to other boats on the same berth. The advice of some fishermen

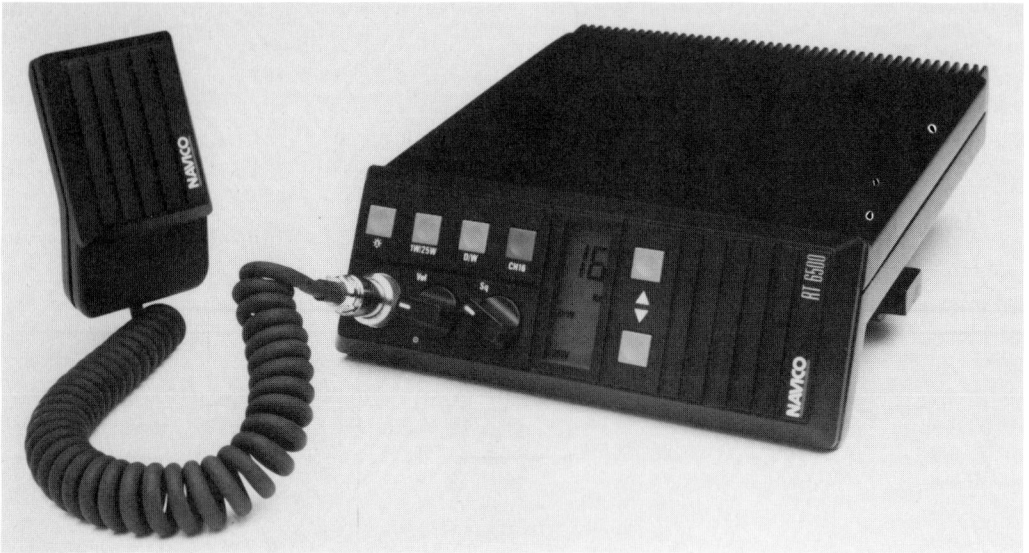

When approaching a marina or harbour call the harbour or port control on your VHF radio where the authorities will direct you to a berth or mooring.

When approaching a strange harbour, study the chart for any anomalies such as foul areas, lights, special marks. On approach, look out for speed limit or direction signs.

should be treated with a touch of caution, not so much because of their cavalier attitude to visiting yachts, but because of the difference in their view of boats. Trawlers are generally rugged, on the best berths and held away from the wall by huge fenders. The fishermen are not concerned about the occasional knock and the boats are – anyway – built to take it. Cruisers are different.

The most usual hazards in a drying berth are:

1   A ledge, or horizontal timber, projecting from the wall at about half-tide level.
2   Vertical pilings at the same water-level.
3   Rough ground, stones, footings and rubbish close to the wall.
4   Ground which slopes very steeply away from the foot of the wall.
5   Very thick, very soft mud.
6   A tidal surge which causes a swell, or a run, at certain stages of the flood.
7   Wash from regular ferries, tugs, trawlers, etc.

These are the things you should be asking about, as well as enquiring about facilities and charges. These latter might be nil, but some of the greedier areas of southern Britain charge very high fees for a trawler-plagued drying berth, with no such facilities as water, electricity, bollards, drains, showers, toilets and convenient ladders. If you find one of these demanding £10 per night for a 9m (30ft) yacht, you will get a better bargain in a deep-water port or the nearest marina.

Marina Berthing

Even though many people regard marina berthing as an easy, soft option, it does not relieve you of the skipper's essential need for detailed operational planning and can – on occasions – be a very demanding feat of seamanship. If you doubt this last observation, take station and watch at your own marina on any Sunday evening. Fortunately, making a right Charlie of coming to a pontoon rarely causes serious damage, and even dramatic errors are often diminished and rapidly rectified by a bit of neighbourly muscle.

If the marina is well staffed, it is both erroneous and discourteous to arrive and merely grab a berth without guidance. A VHF call on the appropriate channel often brings a bonus. On a recent club cruise, most members dived in close to the end of the pontoon, where they were a considerable distance away from the facilities and vulnerable to passenger-ferry wash. The couple of boats who called in were guided up to super berths belonging to absent locals and – because they knew they were arriving – the marina staff came down to take the warps and to offer the local brochure and advice.

Let's Go In

If you have made radio contact with the marina staff and have been allocated a berth, you will also know whether you will be port side or starboard side to the pontoon, and can be well prepared in advance. If not, you may have to consider getting fenders and warps out for both sides.

Our own policy is firstly to look at the wind. We have a high-sided, high wind-age boat, but have no real apprehensions about taking on tight manoeuvres to get into a good berth. Our on-board discussion of priorities is:

1   Can we get a berth 'headish' to wind to give the comfort of a sheltered cockpit?
2   Can we find a berth where the wind will blow us onto the pontoon as we come alongside? (We have actually done this in strong winds, then later warped across the gap so that the wind held the boat off the pontoon, which is much better for hull protection.)
3   If we cannot locate a berth to suit our plans, we motor right down to the end of the pontoon rows to have a look at the options, then either reverse back to the chosen slot, or turn short round in the 'lane' and come back ahead.

Marina Reversing

Many owners rightly get edgy about their own safety when they see another boat reversing between the pontoons. In our own typical case, the deepest point of draught is well astern, so the bow is greatly affected by wind. Even though we are going astern, 'watch the bow' has to be a priority.

Progress is a mixture of force and gentleness. Because the rudder will not work unless the boat has sufficient astern steerage way, we can keep control only by a series of bursts on the engine and total concentration to stay on line. From time to time, we need to go ahead a touch to bring the swinging bows back into line, and may have to reposition if a very strong side wind blows us completely across the free space between the pontoons.

As long as you do not let your concentration slip, making a long leg astern is easier to do than to describe. It also has to be admitted that there is no substitute for practice and experience.

The Short Turn

Making a 180-degree turn between the lines of pontoons closely resembles the driving test's three-point turn, except that the ends of the boat will slide sideways. To execute it well, you really must know how your propeller makes the hull swing.

Every boat is a variant of our own, with its left-hand prop making her turn to starboard more easily going ahead, whilst the stern kicks hard to starboard in reverse. This means that an anticlockwise turn is considerably easier than turning starboard round.

Because the bow and stern continue their circling motion, without too much linear progress when the engine is put into neutral, this 'evolution' is made with a series of very firm engine bursts. Get over to the right-hand side of the lane, then go firmly half ahead to port. Cut the engine and watch the turn continue. When she is nearly across, go half astern and watch the way she still swings.

We can get round in not much more than our own length – as will any boat with adequate power. This includes right-hand propeller boats, which simply reverse all of the moves above.

Getting into the Slot

The worst way to get into a marina berth is with the boat 'on the swing'. Lightweight boats get away with it by having some human muscle on the pontoon. Cruiser weights and above really must get roughly fore and aft in the same alignment as the finger, especially if they are short-crewed. This might be fiddly to do and you might have to back off to get onto the best line, but patience in manoeuvring is an essential seamanship technique.

The skipper berthing 'on the swing' needs his wits about him to check the tail wag when necessary.

We are always asking if the fenders will bear.

It is also vital to have plenty of fenders, not only out on the correct side, but also low enough to bear on the pontoon. You cannot have too many – including a loose one to be jammed in if you make an error of judgement.

The cruising couple will generally be best advised to put long, light warps out immediately (they are easier to handle), then to put their shorter, heavier-duty ropes on later. A good system is to have one crew member just aft of the bow to get ashore as soon as possible, where a temporary line is made fast. At the helm position, the 'driver' should have a boat hook ready, plus a light line to loop through the eye as soon as he can.

These lines merely pull the boat in. However, because most boats are longer than the finger pontoons, the real urgency is to get a rope where it will stop the boat

Get the crew ashore as early as possible.

from going ahead and 'nose butting' the catwalk pontoon. We are all obsessed with bow ropes, although a line running aft from a midships cleat is often the most important one.

A most useful piece of gear is a very heavy-duty snap shackle on a rope equal to about 75 per cent of the boat's length. This can be tied off to a mid-boat cleat before you dock. If the shore crew immediately gets this onto the fixture at the end of the pontoon, the engine can be left ticking over in forward gear and will hold the craft against the berth until you get sorted out.

This DIY item is so handy that we shall use two of them next year, purely as quick snap-ons to hold us in position until we get ourselves more permanently organized. Fortunately, in most marinas how you actually attach the boat to the pontoon is self-explanatory.

A hook on a warp about 60 to 70 per cent of the boat's length is a very useful berthing tool.

The security of two head warps onto the catwalk.

Two head ropes onto the catwalk to prevent her going backwards, plus a line from the bow, or better still from amidships to the end of the finger to restrain progress ahead, then a breast rope from cockpit to pontoon will usually suffice.

Marina Manners

There are a number of kind acts and politenesses that other people have offered to us and that may be worth your own consideration.

1   To walk across to assist an in-coming yacht is a very friendly act. True, there are some crews who get 'huffy' and consider this an affront to their ability. No matter.

Even though we are reasonably competent, it is always a pleasure to see a fellow cruiser walk out onto the pontoon.

His presence is not only physically helpful to take ropes, but if he is standing close to the end of the finger, he also assists the skipper to orientate the tip which, in our case, vanishes beneath the bluff bow and wheel-house window sill about 6m (20ft) before we hit it. You also make a lot of nice new friends this way.

2   A first task is to 'frap' your halyards so that they do not rattle against the mast. It is not always sufficient to use a rubber bungy. In strong winds, take them from masthead to the sides of the boat.

3   Step gently down from boat to finger. A huge leap might look macho, but it

Tie off your halyards well clear of the mast.

A coiled rope left at the side of the pontoon is neat and allows a smooth unberthing procedure.

makes an impolite din and could cause the other boat to lurch just as its skipper is putting the soldering iron to a very delicate piece of electronics.

4 Have a look at the ends of your mooring lines. Could they be coiled so that nobody trips over them? Hosepipe? Shore power lead? Can much of the spare be pulled back on board?

5 Late-night parties and evening music are great – unless you are an adjacent boat with plans to slip the berth at 0300 next morning.

Marina manners are merely a matter of selfishly thinking about yourself, then transferring these prejudices to how others think of you.

SUMMARY

- Putting a boat to a berth shows up the men from the lads.

- The wind always will be a major factor in deciding where you will berth and which side you will put to the wall.

- Forget about the bow. Pick up your buoy amidships.

- You should be prepared to use the dinghy to get to your buoy and to pick it up in big tides, or large waves.

- The golden rule: when coming alongside, line up as early as possible.

- The warp to amidships cleat is a great finger pontoon boat stopper.

- Warps and springs stretch slightly, but their prime function is to keep you close in and exactly where you want to be, even when the tide goes up and down.

- Alongside other boats, you still put your own warps onto the shore or onto the mooring buoy.

- Taking the ground is easy, but is only completely safe if the boat has been designed for this.

- Think of others. Will you need to walk across their boat? Do your halyards tap? Neighbours also like to sleep.

6
UNBERTHING

Whether or not the opposite of berthing is 'unberthing' could be open to semantic debate, but the word exactly describes the process of getting the boat away from where she has been secured to the land, or even to another vessel.

Fortunately, unberthing is a much simpler business than putting the boat into a bed for the night, but it still has to be planned. The increasing use of marinas also reduces the difficulty, the planning and the amount of sheer physical effort that might be needed to get the hull to come unstuck from the quay.

About 90 per cent of unberthing moves involve moving the boat astern, so this is where we shall concentrate our efforts.

The skipper's prime objective must always be to get the boat out with the bow facing the way he wishes to go. On occasions, one loses patience with those owners who complain, 'Going astern, this boat always goes the way she wants. In reverse, she has a mind of her own.' That is really nonsense. With a bit of thought, any boat can be backed out of a marina slot and made to point towards the easy exit.

Most of the complainants are reluctant to use springers and warps to dictate terms to the boat. Many have retained the dinghy philosophy of cast off and go, whereas they ought to be developing big-ship habits: no manoeuvre close to a quay can be accomplished without planning, communication and external aids.

There are skippers who feel that using extra lines to get away from a quay implies some sort of confession of poor boat handling. To me, such misplaced pride is an admission of foolishness. A good skipper will always accept – indeed is always actively seeking – any means to make his life easier and to protect both his own boat and those of others from possible damage.

Having made the point that life is not always a simple matter of flash up the engine, cast off and go, let us have a look at some specific problem situations and the remedies.

Tidal Treguier

A couple of years back, we motored up-river to Treguier and were very surprised to find it to be very uncrowded, even though it was a Saturday in July. The Capitaine du Port told us, 'We are always short of visitors for this weekend. This is the biggest tide of the year and when the ebb combines with the river, we get a very strong current passing through the pontoons. You will want your best ropes here.'

The next day, his point was reinforced as a number of yachts tried to leave to take the ebb down river and were simply flung sideways onto the sterns of those moored opposite, as they tried to pass between the pontoon rows. It got so bad that you dared

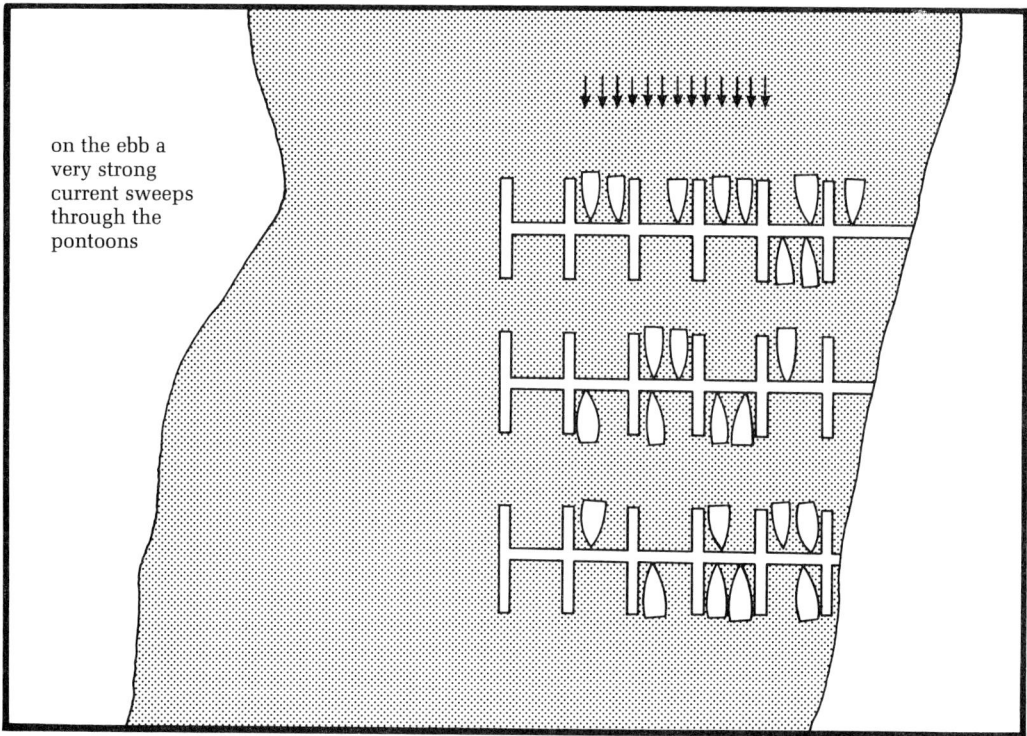

on the ebb a very strong current sweeps through the pontoons

Treguier, where river current and tide cause problems at times.

not leave your own boat unattended and one unfortunate was so pinned that both crews had to spend a whole two hours keeping the boats apart until the tide eased.

Our departure was planned for 1000 on Tuesday morning, when the tide should just begin to move down towards the sea again. On Monday evening, we took the decision to be prudent cowards and, on the slack water, vacated our berth with the bows up-stream, to take station in a slot on the end of the up-stream line of pontoons with our bows facing down, where the flood would come from.

The next morning, during the last quarter of an hour of a flood-tide that we could see weakening by the minute, we pulled our lines inboard and simply let the flowing water drop us astern away from the finger pontoon. We did not even need the engine. Thereafter, we enjoyed forty minutes of slack water, then a roaring ebb ride for the rest of the way.

The incident is recalled because it highlights a number of unberthing factors. You need to think about it. Prudence is good seamanship. You must try to utilize any natural forces that are available.

The Simple Stern Spring

Our skipper who moans that the boat has a

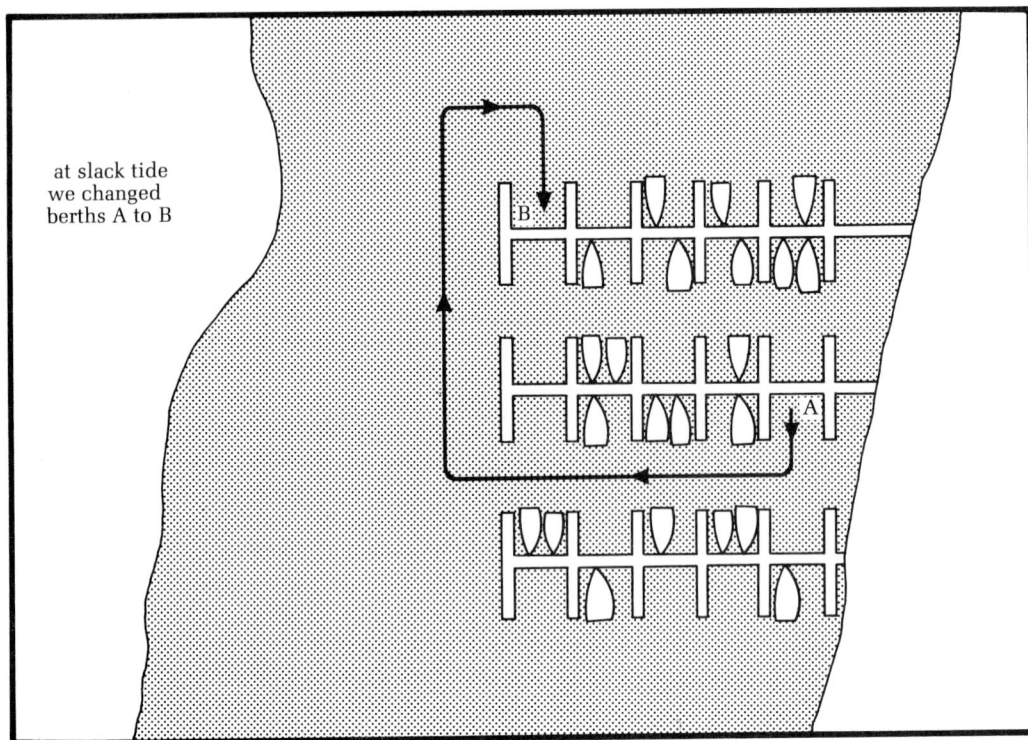

The Treguier manoeuvre to cheat the tide.

at slack tide
we changed
berths A to B

mind of its own could control that mind with a simple piece of rope. Supposing he wishes to exit a marina berth and to turn his stern to port, leaving his bow swinging to starboard ready to move off to the end of the pontoon in that direction.

He simply needs to cleat one end of a warp to his own port quarter, loop it through a ring on the end of the finger and take a turn round a cockpit winch with the free end. The rope can be allowed to slip, but as soon as the stern is clear, or the bows are sufficiently backed out to swing clear of the obstructions to starboard, putting a check on the springer will swing her tail to port. It would be prudent to get the crew to watch the bow *vis-à-vis* the next

boat, but if the bow swinging is too sharp, the spring can be let run and the swing eased.

When she is sufficiently out in the channel, the looped warp can be retrieved inboard.

The Piggy-back Spring

It could be argued that if the wind is pinning you so hard against the finger pontoon that getting away is a problem, you probably ought not to be going to sea. However, it happens quite regularly to low-powered boats, or to the smaller cruiser powered by an outboard motor.

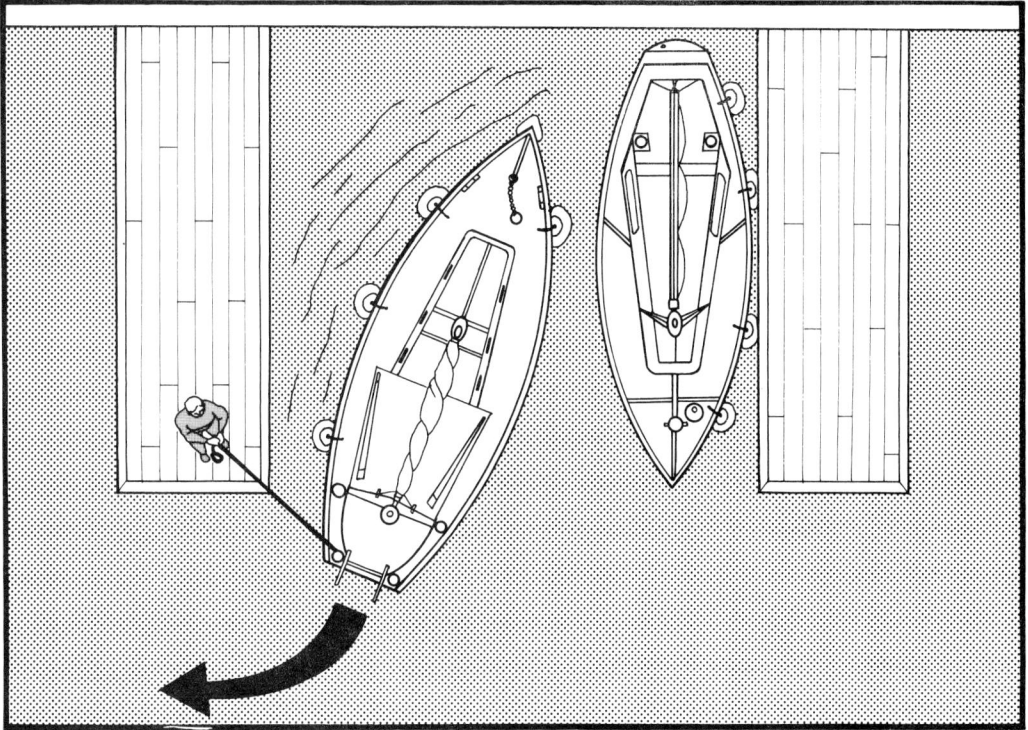

Reversing out of the berth on a stern springer.

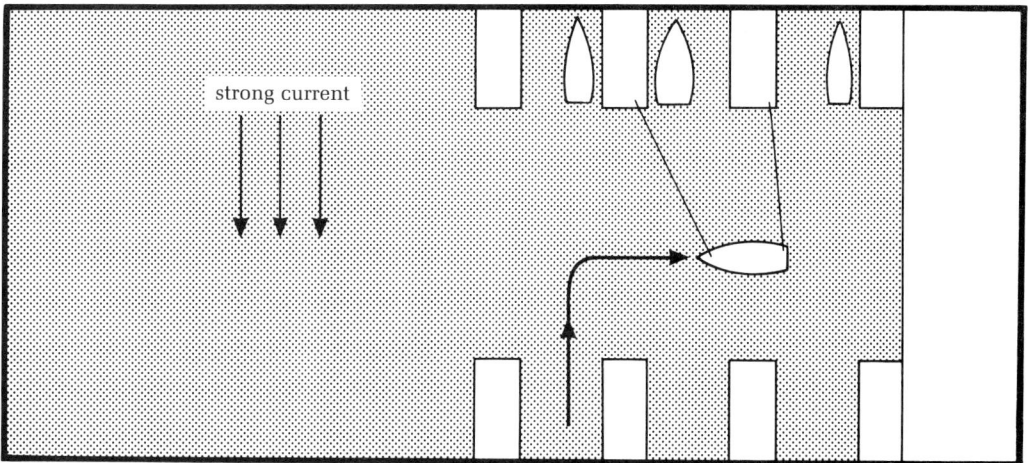

strong current

Get a margin of safety by warping across to the next finger pontoon – even if it is occupied.

Logic dictates that you must give yourself a bit of room, by getting the boat upwind away from the pontoon to which you are being pinned. Fortunately, most double pontoon rectangles are so narrow that you can easily get a couple of doubled ropes across to the up-wind finger and bodily winch your boat sideways towards it.

If the other berth is occupied, get permission to loop your warps around his winches, or a convenient cleat. Before you call around to ask, though, just satisfy yourself that your neighbour has put out mooring warps that are sufficient to take the double weight. You are unlikely to do him any harm if he is secured 'good and square'. Firstly, the wind will be blowing him off the pontoon. Secondly, your weight will try to pull him even further.

Getting away from a lee berth is such a common occurrence that many commercial

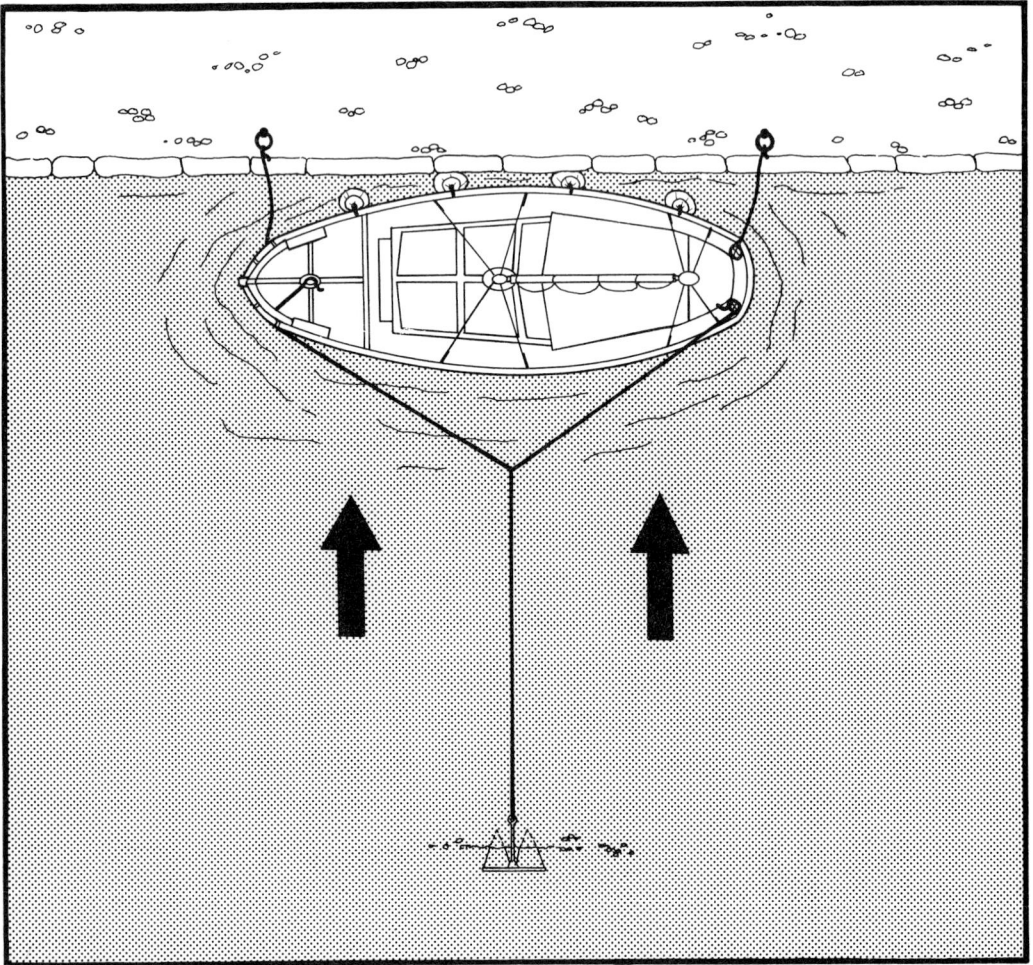

The holding-off anchor.

harbours lay special mooring buoys about 30m (98ft) out from the quay. Big ships run warps to them so that they can pull themselves broadside to get clear.

Professionals also execute a very classy manoeuvre in which they drop a bow anchor (sometimes even bow and stern) a little distance off as they let a combination of wind, engine and bow thruster drift them alongside. The anchors will be used to pull them off again. In very extreme conditions, even yachts have taken the kedge out in the dinghy to do the same thing.

That's Cruising

Only rarely will you be forced into such extreme action, either to get out of a berth, or even to hold yourself away from a wall onto which you are being hounded by wind and waves. In that situation most of us would either try to moor bows out on the anchor and stern in to the wall, or look for a slot elsewhere.

That is the beauty of cruising. It is mostly a safe adventure in which you please yourself when to come, to go, or to remain.

SUMMARY

- 90 per cent of unberthing involves moving the boat astern.

- The prime objective is to get the boat out with the bow facing the way the skipper wishes to go.

- Using extra lines can make life easier and will protect the boat from possible damage.

- Prudence is good seamanship. Utilize any natural forces which are available.

- Use a simple stern spring to swing the stern to port.

- When using the piggy-back spring get permission from the occupier of the other berth to loop your warps around his winches.

- Commercial harbours often lay special mooring buoys to assist in getting away from a lee berth.

7

THE AMATEUR PROFESSIONAL

'If we are going to do it, then let us do it properly.'

This statement is the business philosophy of one of the most successful and wealthy men I know. In effect, it is saying that shoddy knowledge and an unwillingness to give each project sufficient time and money are the path to failure. Time looks after itself; the money needs to be thought about and spent on things to make the boat better – rather than just flashier.

The Cordage Locker

'A ship is as good as her ropes' is a seaman's traditional truism. It is amazing that people will spend £100,000 on a boat, but will begrudge a couple of hundred for the ropes to make her safe. A walk around any harbour, or a paddle around an anchorage, is revealing and worrying. String rather than good ropes seems to be the fashion aboard some vessels, with cheap and nasty blue polypropylene to the fore. In calm weather it holds. In rough weather it breaks.

A cruising boat needs a minimum of four long mooring warps (bow, stern and two springers), at least one of which should be long enough and strong enough to act as a tow rope. My own preference would always be for at least two of these to be long enough to double through a ring and come back to the boat even in enormous tides.

These mooring warps should be of nylon – plaited nylon is great – because its stretch and elastic properties lessen the damage done by snatching when the boat is moored in windy or other surging conditions. All of your warps should be accessible in a hurry.

We also have a number of long, light lines, which are mostly ex-halyards, having a number of uses from acting as easy-to-use temporary mooring warps, to rigging as safety lines for crew harnesses. We also have four short 8m (26ft) very heavy-duty warps for attaching the boat to a mooring buoy, or for fore and aft berths between piles.

Our luxury rope is 60m (197ft) of good, strong climbing rope picked up very cheaply from a car-boot sale. It is not used very often, so is simply fed down into a canvas bag, so that it will 'run' out if we pull the free end, or if we keep an end on board and row the bag away in the dinghy.

This is an emergency rope. It has pulled other boats out of dangerous places too far for a 'tug' to reach, been used to recover trailers and to warp a dinghy in to a very windy lee shore, and has even been

Coiled into a bag, it comes out again without kinks.

stretched between mooring and quay when it was too windy to row the dinghy.

Like all warps, it will be thrown away if it ever gets chafed badly enough to need knotting, and it benefits from an annual freshwater bath. In the same sort of bag, we also have a couple of lengths of chain, which serve to hold us on mooring buoys in a real blow, or to put on the kedge in less ferocity.

Towing

If you go your whole cruising life without towing, or being towed, you will indeed be fortunate. The main decision is whether to conduct the operation with the boats alongside each other, or in line astern.

Out at sea, if possible, you always tow astern on a line that is long enough for comfort and for the reduction of snatch caused by waves. Strong and stretchy are the descriptive words for a towline and you may even need to put a heavy weight half-way between the vessels. Once under way, it is the duty of the casualty to steer straight enough to be directly behind the tug at all times. Sheering about reduces the forward pull and increases the strain on both vessels.

In harbour you may have to lash the boats together. This needs plenty of thought, to position and balance the casualty so that he has the least 'rudder' effect

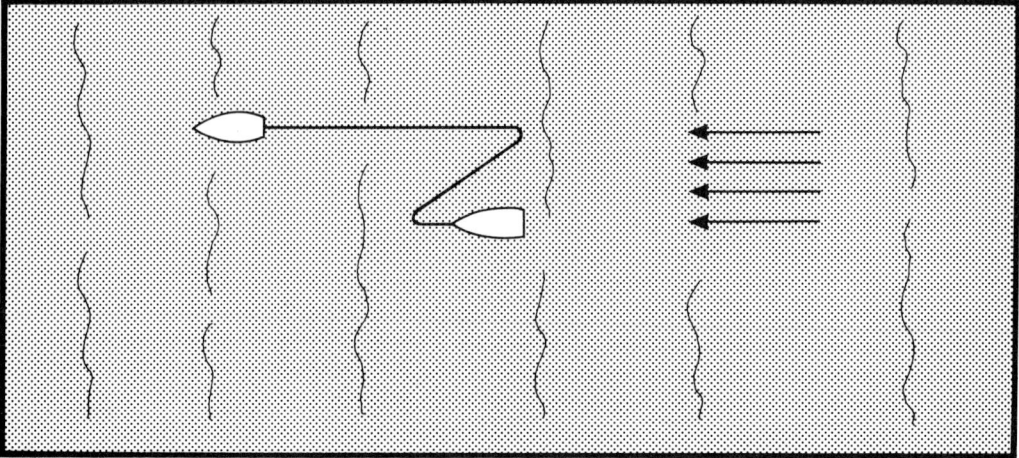

Danger is the tow overtaking the tug.

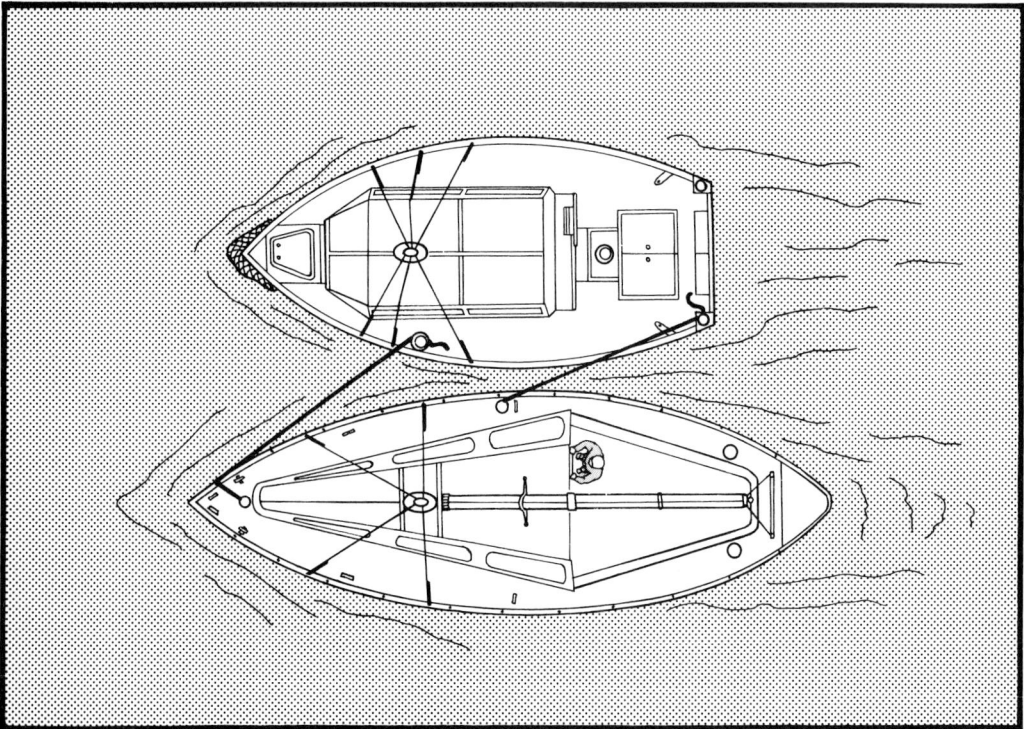

Ropes placed correctly for towing alongside.

on the tug. Water resistance will always pull the tug sharply towards the towed boat, and makes turning the pair away from the captive hull very difficult.

It is best accomplished with two ropes from well forward of the tug to points 66 per cent forward and about 20 per cent forward of the casualty. Before putting ropes on, imagine what their effect will be. Here you are getting the best pull points to maximize straight-line efficiency and preventing the towed boat from veering away. You will also need a breast rope to hold his bow in and have him steer towards you to reduce the drag effect, which always tries to turn you both away. This effect will be amplified in both directions if there is a strong wind, i.e. it will blow you even

The useful tugboat hitch.

more onto the dead weight and offer greater resistance when you try to turn into it.

This operation is also another argument in favour of the biggest dinghy and outboard you can manage. A good one can be lashed alongside and used to move a crippled parent boat.

Towing Knots

The tugboat hitch is particularly effective and very under-used by amateurs. Knots such as the clove hitch are impossible to get off if they have been snatched tight, and are even worse when wet. Because the tugboat hitch is merely passed as a loop beneath the towline and dropped over the bollard, it never tightens on itself. Two successive loops will hold most loads, and it is so effective that we even use it to make our halyards tight and safe around deck winches.

What Flag is She?

If a boat is as good as her ropes, she will often be known and respected by her flags.

Most of us need to pause for observation of the entrance before we enter a strange marina. That should be the time to check and to set the flags. By law, you must fly the ensign of your country of origin when entering or leaving a foreign port during the hours of daylight. You will also give the impression of being a 'well-found little ship' if your house, courtesy and Q flags are in the proper place and order.

Many marina limpets make a sport of sniffing at those who want the kudos and ego of flying a string of flags and burgees, but are too lazy to do the research to fly them correctly.

1   The correct national flag for British-registered craft is the Red Ensign (certainly not the Union Jack or the EC Stars), which should be flown at the aftermost point or on the mizzen mast.

The Royal Navy and the Royal Yacht Squadron, plus boats with a serving RN officer aboard, wear the White Ensign. Some clubs and associations have a special warranty to fly an undefaced Blue Ensign, or the defaced version with the club symbol at the fly.

2   Club burgees and special designs, or house flags, should really be flown at masthead, but modern electronics creates so much clutter at the top of the mast, that the practice of flying them at the cross trees is quite general. The starboard yard-arm should be used if possible, with the flag of the most senior club at the top. There is usually a bit of room for debate about this.

3   Unfortunately, that same yardarm is the 'official' site for any courtesy ensign to be flown. These are the smaller flags of any foreign country you are visiting. To get over the problem, the polite method is to reduce the status of your own pennants to the port spreaders, whilst giving your host country's flags pride of place to starboard. The precedence is national over regional, i.e. the French tricolour above the black and white hermines of Brittany, or superior to the Normandy leopards.

4   Dressing the ship overall is polite on such official occasions as (a) a British national festival (b) a foreign festival (c) a local festival – but it is also permissible fun to celebrate purely 'on-board' occasions such as birthdays and anniversaries.

5   The yellow flag Q, announcing that your vessel is healthy and requesting free pratique (clearance by Customs), should be flown as soon as you cross the boundary of international waters into claimed territorial space (12 miles when returning to the UK) and should currently be left aloft until you have delivered your 'nothing to declare' form to the local HM Customs box. If you have goods to declare, leave it up.

NB   Some countries (e.g. France) do not require the display of flag Q by visiting pleasure craft, unless they have specific goods to declare, or are otherwise in contravention of local laws concerning such things as the amount of hard currency on board. Marine almanacs are one source of information, and the appropriate embassies are another.

There is no designated, official hoist for flag Q. The regulations simply state that it shall be flown 'in a conspicuous place', both day and night.

Legal and seamanship regulations apart, we fly club and association flags because we like to show that we belong and because it is fun, but once you get away from your own cruising patch, your marine badges take on a more practical role.

In Cherbourg, for instance, our Auxiliary Coastguard flag brought a number of visitors, including a fellow member whom I had not met for years and would have missed without the flag. Similarly, at La Coruña we called to say hello to another member of the Cruising Association and were able to dive to free his anchor, which was stuck in a mooring chain. Without the flag, there would have been no visit – only a £120 bill for a Spanish diver.

Sound Signals

There are occasions when you are pleased

Auxiliary coastguards fly their own flag.

—	I am turning to stbd.	— — .	I shall overtake to st'bd
— —	I am turning to port	— — . .	I shall overtake to port
— — —	My engines are going astern	— . — .	I understand your intentions.
— — — —	Your intentions are not clear.	————	Approaching a sharp bend.

You can make your own chart of sound signals.

that you have an easy recall of ship's sound and siren signals. They are simple to commit to memory, if you tie them to the logic of the Rules of the Road. The first rule is that you shall keep to starboard – so, one sound blast means 'I am directing my course to starboard'. Two blasts tells you that he is turning to port – red to red would be the second option. Three blasts announce 'I am operating astern propulsion'. This does not always mean that he is making way astern, but could be telling you that the engine has been reversed to stop the boat.

A whole series of blasts is a warning that you are a hazard, or that a dangerous situation is about to develop, so watch out and keep clear. This is sometimes described as the 'I am in doubt about you, so wake up' signal. The other problem signals are the morse code letter Uniform – dit, dit, dah – which signifies 'Your vessel is running into danger'; and its opposite cluster Delta – dah, dit, dit – to say 'I am manoeuvring with difficulty, so keep clear'.

The Ship's Logbook

There are a number of very good reasons for keeping a ship's log. The first and most important is that it is an official document, which could be asked for should you ever be caught up in any sort of enquiry. The second is the very sensible practicality of noting things down so that you do not forget them. When did you last pump the bilges? At what time are you due to turn down a grease gland again? Where were you twenty minutes ago? If you know, you will be able to start navigating again if the electronics fail.

This last will happen only if you have kept a note of your course, speed, track over the ground, the mileage on the log read-out and the wind, weather and visibility. There are a number of patent logbooks on the market, but none of them seems to suit us all, so many people end up designing their own. Ours is on loose leaf, which can be used double sided – one for waypoints and electronics and the other for a running commentary on the trip.

The log is also a good *aide-mémoire* for later on – when you wish to know how many engine hours you have done in a season, or how much fuel you have passed through the tank, or to save yourself the labour of working out the latitude or longitude of waypoints that you have already used the year before.

The Cruising Log

One of the more pleasurable winter evening activities is to spend an hour or so with our own, personal cruising log. This is a stiff-covered book, in which the right-hand page contains just a few lines about where we were and what we did each day, plus a short note of what we spent and who we met. The left-hand side is reserved for a selection from the photographs that we take.

It is surprising how soon you either forget, or merge one pleasurable excursion into another. The cruising log is one of our better inventions. Most of us need to work and to save very hard in order to secure our cruising freedoms, so what a shame if time is allowed to dim the memory of our best moments.

SUMMARY

- A boat is usually as good as its cordage.

- You cannot have too many ropes – but they must be good – not knotted polypropylene.

- Ideally a tug boat should be heavier than its tow. If not try lashing him alongside.

- Learn the tugboat hitch. Very useful.

- The bowline is the other essential knot.

- Flag etiquette: some find it fussy, others see it as the mark of a good seaman.

- Sound signals are very logical and follow the rules of the road.

- Valuable documents: the ship's log and a cruising diary log.

- Keep all your cruise/navigational information ready for next year – especially if you got it right.

- The good skipper has two mottos (1) If he's bigger get out of the way. (2) If we're going to do it let's do it properly.

When towing another craft, a useful knot for securing the tow line is the tugboat hitch. When towing always be wary of the tow overtaking the tug.

8
GET THE
RIGHT EQUIPMENT

This section is in some senses a piece of author's self-indulgence. We all tend to be a bit different (fortunately) in what we consider to be essential, on-board equipment. We all (unfortunately) occasionally get a bee in the bonnet and purchase an item of gear that turns out to be utterly useless. This chapter, then, is an attempt to protect your wallet, whilst making your life at sea safer, more efficient and a great deal more fun.

The suggestions below are offered because they have worked for us, or have given us a deal of pleasure. Our lifestyle demands a very comprehensively equipped boat, because some of the places we go to are a bit remote, but we still have to live and to work on board. In a normal season, we join the shake-down cruise with the local club in April, then load up and depart south as soon as we can get our work, our domestic lives, our finances and the boat sorted out. We live aboard in France and Spain until August, then return for the club's bank holiday cruise, before finishing our season in Normandy, where we start our shopping for the next season to come. This itinerary is quoted to show the background against which we prepare our own boat, in the hope that our experience will enable you to select equipment to suit your particular style of cruising and perhaps inspire you to add suggestions of your own.

The items described below were not all purchased at once, but that is also part of the cruising pleasure. Our boat is ashore for the winter, but this does not mean that cruising becomes a dead hobby – even without the winter maintenance and improvement plan. Every time we go on a weekend shopping expedition, we buy a couple of things for the boat: a few stainless steel screws here and a shackle there; a cassette tape today and a packet of dough mix to make fresh English bread in Spain tomorrow.

Other items are put onto a birthday and Christmas present list. By the time of the festive season, we already have the new almanacs, some tools, a chart or two and other bits and pieces already wrapped and in the boat's own pile under the tree. In this way we not only spread cruising out to be a year-round pastime, but buy the equipment as we think of it and in a manner that better suits our limited finances.

Come April, we are always very glad that we already have a spare cupboard full of edible goodies, plus a very large box of spares ready to load. By following a system of deferred payments over the winter, we are not suddenly presented with the sort of bill that hurts, just to get the ship up to scratch again. Besides, it is fun.

Turning a new boat into into a properly personalized, highly efficient cruiser, naturally divides itself into a number of departments. On a big ship, each one would be the responsibility of a particular officer. On a yacht, the whole task of not forgetting something important is down to the owners. They must ensure that they have:

1   Adequate safety equipment
2   The means to transport the gear to the boat
3   The wherewithal to cope with emergencies at sea
4   The supplementary items to make an efficient cruiser
5   Some things to make life aboard a lot of fun.

These sections and the items that they contain are not listed in any order of importance. They are penned as a browse in the hope that you too will browse and make up your own list of what you want and when you will hope to acquire it. We also have to admit to being a belt-and-braces boat – if anything, we have too many spares aboard, if such a state is possible. It is almost a motto in our own club that if an item cannot be found aboard *Abemama*, it probably does not exist.

Safety Equipment

Life-jackets or Buoyancy Aids?

These will necessarily be high on the list of essential safety gear, so we should be clear about the differences between them.

We are really talking about power. A buoyancy aid is more the province of the water-skier and the dinghy sailor. It is designed to assist you to stay afloat and does not have much claim beyond this. It is light and easy to stow.

Full life-jackets are of two sorts, but both are designed to turn the wearer over so that his face is clear of the water and to support him in that position for very long periods. The permanent type comprises a waterproof cover with a filling of very buoyant material. It is undoubtedly the more efficient, but is very bulky to wear, inhibits your movement about the boat and is a real headache to stow. If you are a poor swimmer, this type makes most sense.

The alternative is some sort of inflatable life-jacket, which is generally worn horse-collar style around the neck. The best of them are both tough and light and can be inflated by a small gas cylinder, by mouth, or by both. Whilst it is recognized that anyone can be unconscious as they go overboard, you have to consider other things too. For a competent swimmer, the folding life-jacket is perfectly adequate. In extreme conditions, he can always blow a bit of air into the bag as a back-up.

The marine scene seems to have gone top-heavy (one is tempted to say gone overboard) over life-jackets with pundits screaming because a crew appears on deck without life-jackets, even though it is an absolute flat calm and the boat is motoring along at 2 knots. We all have our own parameters here. Ours is that life-jackets are worn when life looks desperate enough to need them, e.g. we are in big waves and working out on deck, or going from boat to dinghy in marginal conditions.

Children need different considerations.

Safety Harnesses

These also come high on the list. There is plenty of choice in this department and – like buoyancy – they can be separate, or can be incorporated into a heavy-weather jacket.

Emergency Signalling Pack

This comprises flares, a signal mirror, a whistle and a torch. They are all stowed for immediate accessibility and it is a good idea to have to hand a waterproof box (such as a flare container) into which they can all be stuffed if you have to abandon ship. Some skippers leave this emergency box ready packed at all times.

The principles of pyrotechnics are that you need a very bright light, generally well up into the air, to attract attention to the vessel in trouble. This should be followed by a signal of sufficient duration to enable others to pinpoint your position and to take a bearing on it.

Most packs contain sufficient red flares, which is the international distress signal, plus a number of orange smoke burners, which are position fixers and can also show a helicopter the direction and strength of the wind. You should also have some white flares, which are used to identify your boat in non-Mayday conditions and are the recognized signal to indicate to another craft that you have seen him or to warn him off as he is coming too close.

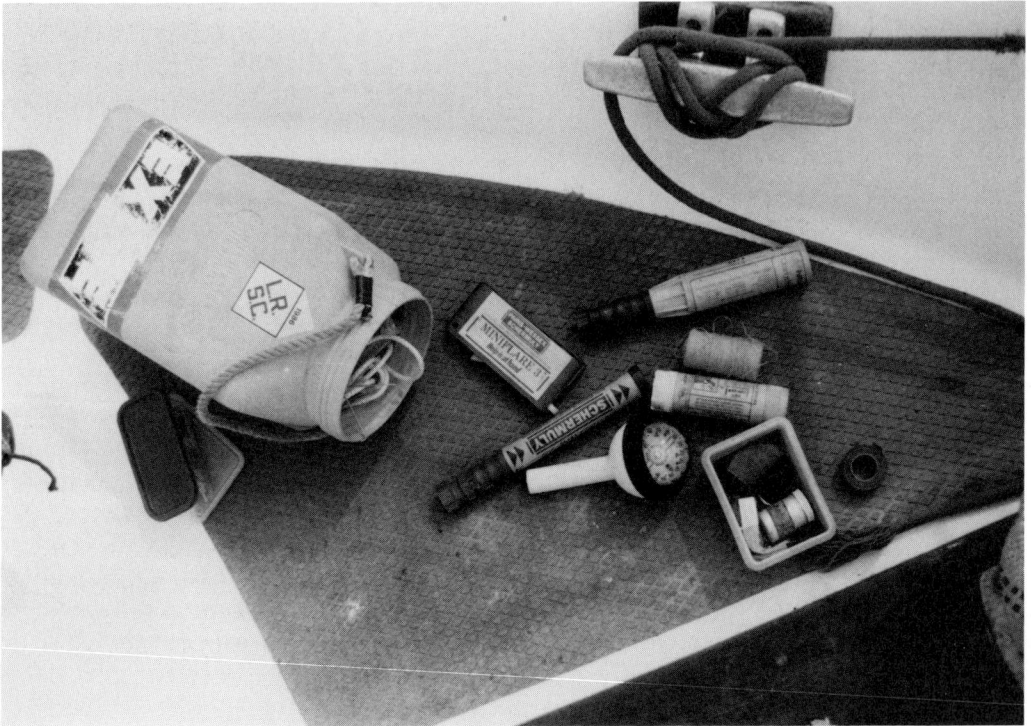

Our panic box contains flares and much besides.

The mini flare is a good stand-by.

The ship's torch – the bigger the better.

We also carry a launcher and a couple of magazines of mini flares – white and red. We have actually used a white to warn a power boat away from our divers and have come close to launching one to show a tanker that we were ahead at night. We keep our out-of-date whites for this very same reason. Out-of-date reds can be buried out in the Hurd Deep, or passed to the local Coastguard or RNLI for use in practice, or for professional disposal.

The most foolish thing to do is to use them as part of a carnival celebration, even well inland. There have been cases of ships out at sea spotting celebratory reds, but having no means of knowing that they had been launched from the shore. The resultant searches by lifeboat and helicopter were expensive and certainly did nothing to enhance the cruising fraternity's reputation for competence.

Spotlight and Torch

These live close to hand in the wheel-house or cockpit. The larger light is driven from the boat's 12v supply and is on a long lead. The torch is waterproof and was obtained from a dive shop, which tends to be marginally cheaper than a traditional chandlery. We also have a charger that will recharge nicad batteries from the boat supply.

The 12v pack powers much else besides the spotlight.

LVM Portable Power Pack

This is a recent addition to our electrical armoury. It is in its own case with a shoulder strap, so it can be moved around the boat. With a payload of 4 ampere hours and a maximum pull of 10 amps, it is a very versatile tool. In its prime mode, it can be taken right up into the bows to run the spotlight as a searchlight for lobster pots, or when coming into strange harbours. We also keep it handy as a powerful light to shine onto our sails at night, or even to fire straight at a boat that looks to be encroaching on our water space. We have used it to run a riding light, to test circuits, to give longer life to our hand-held marine radio and also to run a ham

band's 2m (6.5ft) rig. The pack has also been left coupled up to a flat battery for a couple of hours, and gave it enough life to start the engine. Our version also delivers 6 volts and can be recharged from the ship's batteries.

Portable Pumps

These will also find a dozen uses. We now carry three. One is a hand pump with a long barrel. It can be inserted into odd spaces such as the tiller flat or under the engine bed, and will evacuate a bucket of water in less than ten seconds.

We have a couple of submersible electric pumps, which can also be used in line. One is entirely reserved for the transfer of

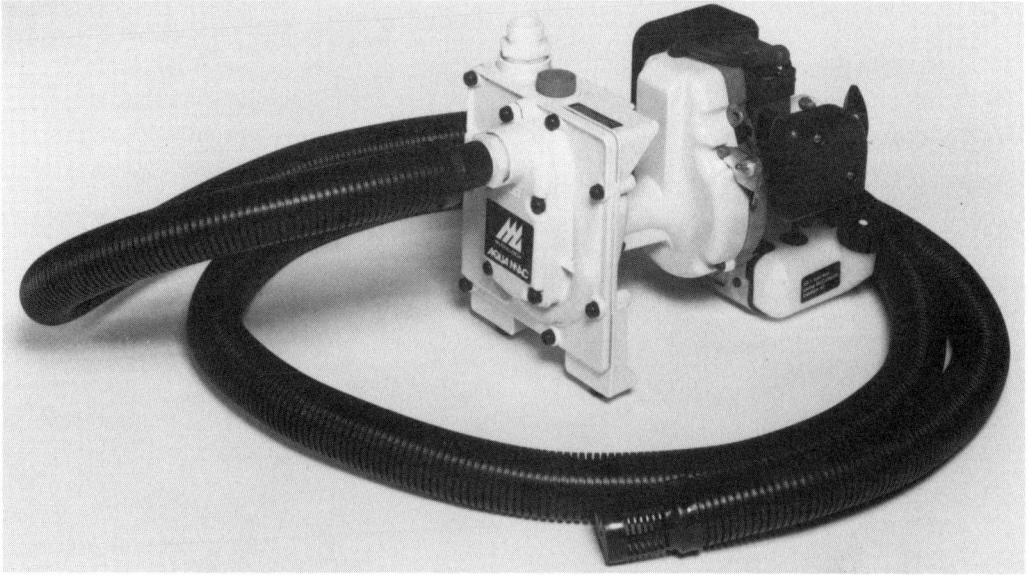

This Aqua Mac portable pump is ideal for the smaller cruiser and can handle up to 1,620 gallons per hour.

Several companies make ranges of buoyancy aids and lifejackets to fit all sizes in the family. These buoyancy aids are marketed by Helly Hansen and are made from puncture-proof closed cell foam.

101

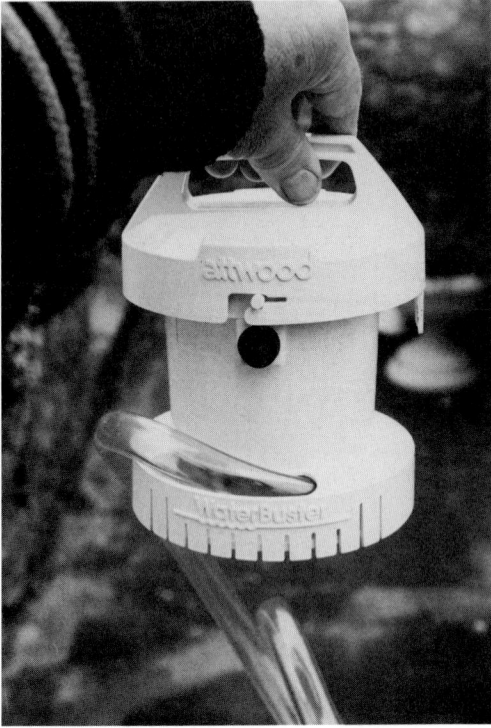

A totally portable pump with rechargeable batteries.

Wood Plugs and Timber

A pack of wood plugs and some odd pieces of patching timber are stowed in a locker, but we hope never to use them. The plugs are a proprietary item from a chandler, the pieces of batten and some scraps of marine ply have been salvaged from various other projects.

Snorkel Mask

This can be leisure equipment, but is equally a safety item. You cannot see well underwater without it, or even look from surface to prop. The mask is the minimum. It would be prudent to add a snorkel tube to facilitate a long examination without repeatedly resurfacing and I would add a set of fins. These are not so much for sheer propulsion, but as an aid to holding you into the side of the boat when you are doing cutting and rubbing jobs. Most water-line and underwater tasks seem to push you away from the hull, so the fins are a good way of retaining pressurized contact.

Suction Gripper

This can be obtained from most chandlers. It adheres very strongly to the hull and is ideal not only for cleaning and inspecting from the dinghy, but will also be a good handgrip when you are reaching under the boat to clear rubbish away from a shallow prop. This definitely goes down as a wise buy on most boats.

Dinghy or Life-raft?

The dinghy versus life-raft debate has continued for a long time. The advantages of a full life-raft are obvious and make a lot of

diesel fuel from the jerrycans to the main tank when we are out at sea. This is convenient, easy and – above all – obviates diesel spillage. The other is a water pump, which can be dropped down into the most awkward places and will pump them dry very efficiently. In a real emergency it would serve as a bilge pump to supplement the manuals and the auto-electric pumps, which are permanently installed.

You can buy cheaper submersible pumps from caravan and camping shops, but will need to check with the manufacturers that they are tough enough to handle diesel and petrol fuels. (We managed to melt our first one.)

The useful suction gripper.

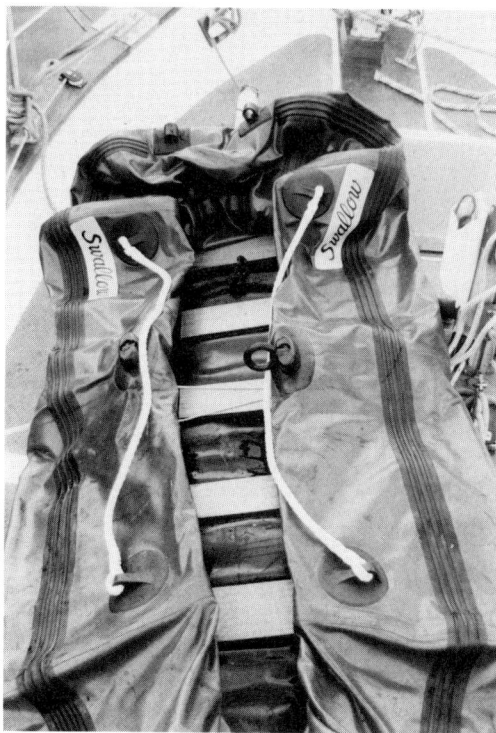

The slatted floor makes for rapid assembly.

sense for blue-water cruisers and racers. The disadvantages are size, enormous cost and a reputation for failure when maximum efficiency really is life or death. Some have failed to open and to inflate on two occasions out of three when they were tried prior to expensive annual overhaul.

Many serious cruising crews do not carry a life-raft. Their reasons are not only those above, but also a feeling that they prefer some sort of motive power. As one told us, 'If I was shipwrecked and drifting past an island in a life-raft, with no means of getting over to it, I could get real mad.' The alternative is a dual-purpose life-raft/dinghy, which can be equipped with a rapid inflation system, or carried partially inflated on deck. There are a number of

inflatable dinghies specifically designed to take a survival canopy. They have a good reputation and have proved very effective when used for real.

Because we have adequate space and a deck protected by deep scuppers, we nowadays carry two inflatables. The large one has floorboards, which are a pain to insert, so we take them ashore and do the job there. Without the floorboards, this boat is vulnerable, floppy and puts pools of water around your feet. In this state, she also underperforms both when rowed and driven by the outboard.

The smaller dinghy has a slatted floor permanently in place. Its rationale is that one year we had to put back into El Ferrol because of bad weather, and were

A small outboard motor like this Evinrude model can be carried to power the ship's tender or dinghy. Choose one with a remote fuel tank which can be disconnected when the engine is laid down.

A folding bicycle can be a boon on board for fetching and carrying stores or just for exploring a new port of call.

hampered because the big dinghy was very securely stowed for seagoing. We were stuck aboard. The smaller one can literally be inflated in two minutes and simply heaved over the side. This gives it some good life-raft potential, and it is a lot of fun if we just want to go messing about or to have a swimming platform. We know one crew who use a similar inflatable as a bathtub.

Outboard Motor

This is included in safety equipment only because it ties in with the inflatable. Here the advice would always be to carry the most powerful engine that you can afford and have the space to stow. One with a remote fuel tank has the advantage of allowing you to pack the tank away separately, especially if you lie the engine down in a locker. Separated, it will not spill fuel and give off fumes in the wrong place. You can also take the remote tank ashore for a refill.

We carry a 3,730-watt (5hp) engine, which is large enough to move the parent boat, and we can tow her both astern and alongside from the dinghy. The engine is light enough for either of us to lift inboard from the dinghy, or to carry reasonable distances up the beach, but is is also powerful enough to get the inflatable up on the plane with two people aboard. This makes sense for long shopping trips, or for day excursions, or for running ahead into strange anchorages to research the area. The combination gives a lot of fun as a taxi for diving and snorkelling, for fishing and setting a small net and has even been used as a tugboat to marina berth a 12m (40ft) whose engine had refused to start.

Transporting the Gear

Rucksacks and Bags

These are an important part of any cruising boat that anchors off, or for those who opt for marinas – most of which are far enough from shops to be inconvenient. Our collection comprises a couple of rucksacks, which we have recently been forced to replace because the straps were not tough enough to take a heavy load. Boat rucksacks have a very hard life, so the better the stitching, the greater the economic sense.

For loading and unloading a cruise boat, there is nothing to beat half a dozen canvas bags with wooden handles. Ours are flat bottomed enough to remain upright in the dinghy, and they serve as temporary, on-board storage until the cruise settles down. But they are also strong enough to take a rope through the handle to cope with high quay walls. They cost a couple of pounds each at a local bazaar.

Boat Bikes

These are also essential carriers. They give us a lot of pleasure when we can get away inland for a day-trip, but are more often used to cart everything, including shopping and jerrycans of diesel fuel, from supplier to ship.

Crews vary in their opinions about bikes. One option are the special marine models, which fold down very small, but have the disadvantage of a very high price tag and inefficiently small wheels – marina runabouts, but very hard work for anything else. We recently met a couple who had two such cycles on board, but they had cost so much that they would not take them out in the rain.

By contrast, we have two ordinary, folding cycles bought as a real bargain from a second-hand dealer. They are of excellent quality, have good big, rolling wheels, will carry a big load and are so cheap that we can afford to replace them after every season, if the need arises. This occasionally happens because, on passage, the cycles live up on the foredeck beneath a couple of canvas sheets and a cargo net – which also has its uses when we berth alongside high walls.

Emergency Repairs

If you never have to make an emergency repair on board, you probably never go to sea. It is an attractive challenge of cruising that the crew will at some time expect to be motor mechanic, sail repairer, electrician, plumber, carpenter, electronics engineer, chef, fibre-glass specialist and several other trades combined. Because the voyager's motto will always be 'Cruising is coping', you must have the necessary items to enable you to deal with all of the foreseeable problems.

The list below is a personal one, but all of the items included have been very valuable at some time or other.

Ascendeur

An ascendeur or some other means of going up the mast is indispensable. Ideally, all members of the crew should be able to go up the stick, but there are certain times when a bit of muscle or DIY skills are needed. Many people are unable to pull a heavy partner up on a deck winch. The alternative is to use the anchor capstan, but this is not always convenient.

Our solution has been to buy a mountain

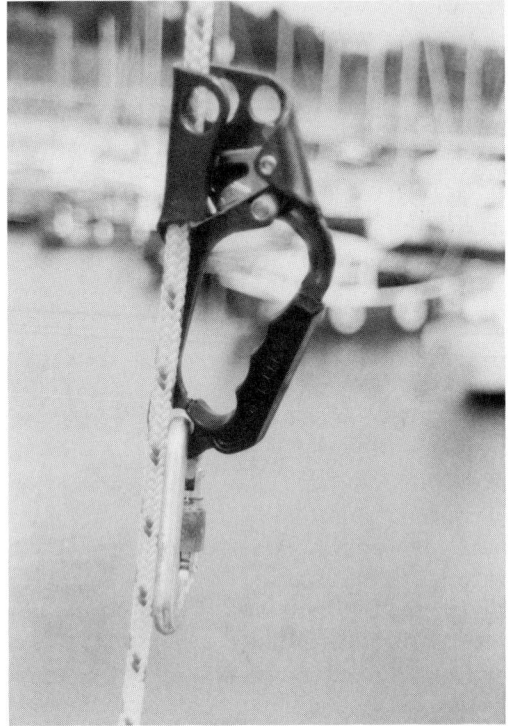

The ascendeur – specialist but sometimes a life saver.

climber's ascendeur, which is a metal device to clamp onto a halyard. It has a patented, toothed brake, which allows the mechanism to be slid upwards, but it locks onto the rope and will not slide down again when the brake is applied.

We winch a spare halyard down as tight as possible and put the ascendeur in place on it. The bosun's chair is attached to another halyard, led back to a deck winch as normal. The climber puts his foot into a loop of rope beneath the ascendeur and slides it up as far as his knee will bend. When he stands up, the weight is taken off the bosun's chair, which is then pulled up tight to his buttocks and takes his weight whilst the ascendeur is slid up another couple of feet. If really pushed, I can get up the mast on my own (two ascendeurs make it even easier), but the system above is very functional and very safe.

Mole Grips and G Clamps

These could possibly be included in the emergency section. Have on board as many as you can afford in terms of cash and stowage space, because any tool that will give a tight and solid, clamping grip will always find a use in temporary repairs. Perhaps temporary is the wrong word, as the two incidents below will illustrate.

Our autopilot's rudder reference unit once detached itself from its mounting plate because I put on too much sail on the fly, instead of turning into the wind. The normal fixing is three self-tapping screws, two of which had vanished. The unit was relocated with one screw, a small G clamp and the ship's molegrips. That happened in May, but the more I looked at the repair, the more it became obvious that it was actually stronger than the original. We cruised the boat very hard until September, with never a murmur of complaint from the rudder reference unit, which had always previously been a source of irritation.

The next time it was the steering cable. We had to make a sudden dodge to avoid a tanker in thick fog off Brittany. At least, I think it was a tanker, but I never actually saw it in my haste to respond to my partner's urgent cry to go left. We did not actually get very far round to port, because the steering cable chose that moment to object to the violent treatment and to part company with the strut of wood against which it is tensioned.

Again, out came the mole grips and G clamps, to effect a repair that was so tight and so impressively superior to the original that, even though we purchased and drilled a stainless steel plate to make good the timber, we went to a market and replaced the ironmongery in order to leave the temporary repair permanently in place until winter. So far it has crossed Biscay twice in some dreadful weather and performed a thousand violent manoeuvres to squeeze the boat into the sort of berth that we always seem to be offered.

Screws and Fuses

Boxes of screws, fuses, etc. are an obvious addition to the locker. Ours are kept in separate, watertight plastic boxes with see-through tops, which just make for easier identification when you are rummaging around in a hurry. A colleague uses boxes of different colours for stainless steel, screws, electrical items and fuses. You simply cannot have too many fuses if your boat has anything like a comprehensive range of electronics. The same can be said of stainless steel nuts and bolts, but a good collection can be built up bit by bit so that the financial shoe's pinch is not even felt.

General-purpose Repair Materials

Those on board include some fibre-glass resin and a few square metres/feet of mat and chopped strand. These have done everything from repairing the heads to attaching bilge pumps to a sloping hull. One of the proprietary **cold weld** compounds is also useful. We have used ours to fix a foot pump in place in the water system, to repair a locker and to put together the kettle's whistle after it had

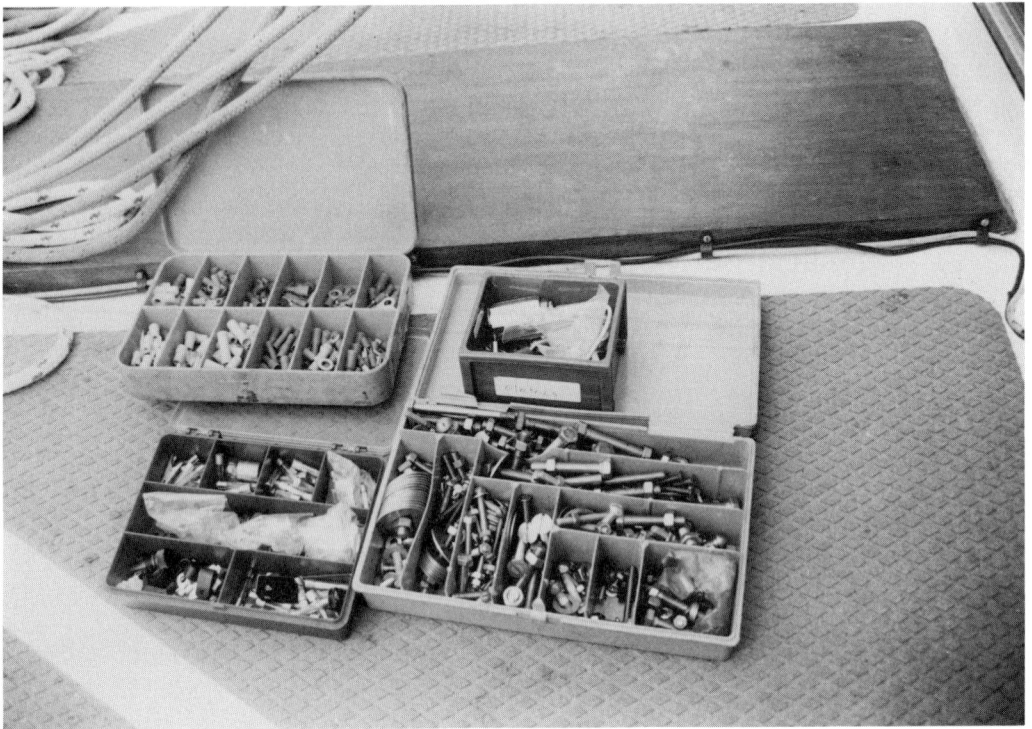

Everything separately boxed for easy storage and access.

blown apart. Several rolls of **insulating tape** find a ready place under the Christmas tree and are constantly in use. Even more useful has been a roll of **pipe repair kit**. This year, ours has been in use to seal an exhaust pipe and, in conjunction with a dab of gasket seal, to effect a temporary repair on a diesel injector. The temporary repair lasted for several months. We also developed a leak on the diesel fuel return pipe (non-pressure side) and were able to seal this with liquid **electrician's insulation**, which is sometimes called black gold and is supplied in a tin complete with its own brush. This is equally excellent in its intended role of sealing electrical connections and making barrier strip aperture water resistant.

Tools

The emergency kit is completed with a variety of wire brushes, major and minor drills, a soldering outfit, the ship's knife and a collection of files, with a Swiss army knife doing everything from supplementary screwdriver duty to cleaning mackerel and being the dinner knife on picnics. On a proper cruiser, the tools are as versatile and adaptable as the people who use them.

Engine Spares

These are a matter of personal faith and preference, and must be dictated by where you cruise. If you plan a foreign trip, you must do the homework to decide which items will be easy to obtain locally and which others could give you considerable problems. On the basis of experience, our spares now have the two major items of spare alternator and starter motor, salvaged from a scrap yard for reconditioning, a spare diesel injector, cylinder-head gasket and water-pump impeller. We have added a couple of injector pipes, some return pipes and a set of copper washers and olives. Even if you cannot fit them yourself, they would all be expensive and time-consuming to have sent from home.

The Efficiency Chest

The equipment detailed below is not all absolutely essential, but its presence can mean the difference between a well-run ship and one that is more difficult to work.

Generator

This regularly proves itself to be a very useful acquisition. We have a 1kw (850-watt continuous) model plumbed into a cockpit locker with an outboard exhaust vent. Run through a relatively cheap battery charger, which will charge at 20 amps, it has once been a miracle worker with a totally dead battery and can also be fired up once a day for thirty minutes to

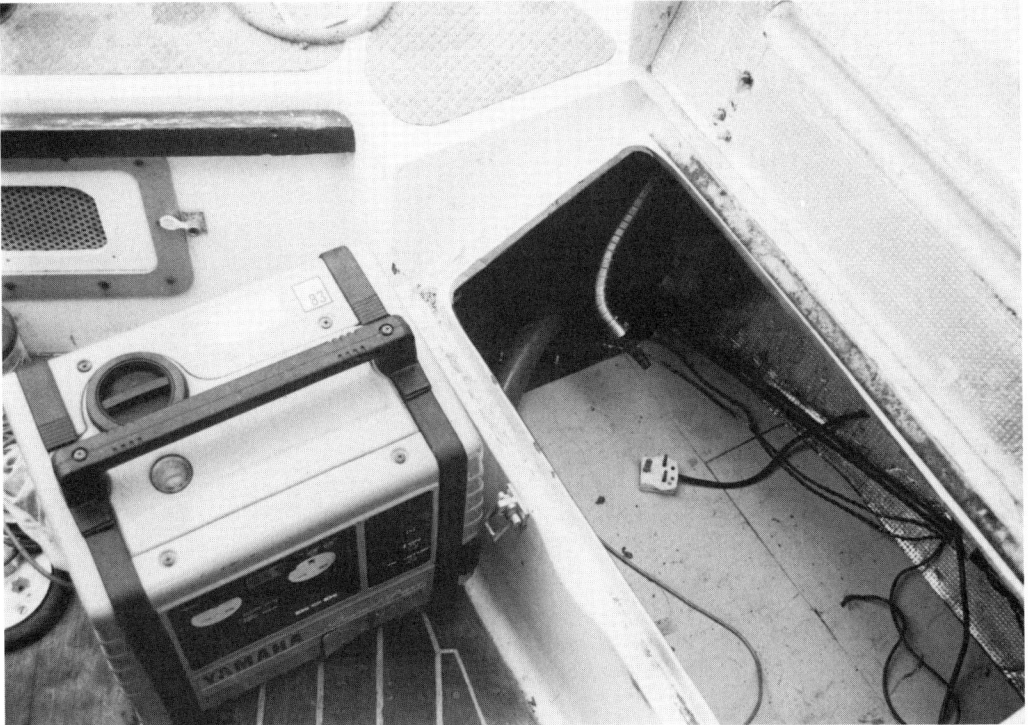

The generator is vented outboard.

recharge the domestic battery bank, rather than put the main diesel through the misuse of running without load. A 220v soldering iron is better than my 12 volter, and the ability to use a full-power electric drill, sander and jigsaw have all been extremely useful on occasions, whilst the low-wattage electric kettle has only once come to our rescue. The genny is, however, one of those items whose absence makes me feel a bit vulnerable.

Mains Lead

A mains lead to bring shore power inboard is a new acquisition. The reasoning is that a lack of anchoring places is increasingly forcing us to use marina berths. As the electricity is included in the fee, we may as well use it for charging batteries (especially if you have a greedy refrigerator with ice maker and freezer compartment) and for running our on-board work computers. If you plan a French trip, buy a continental adaptor to convert to the system which is different from Britain, but universal in mainland continental Europe.

Electrical Tester

An electrical tester or continuity meter regularly proves its worth.

The problem with writing about equipment is that it can be as never ending as its collection is by the cruiser owner. The maxim that 'a boat is as good as its ropes'

would be the source of a whole book in its own right, and we have spent many happy hours making up sail-tying bungy lines – which is certainly cheaper than purchasing them ready made. The ship's first-aid box and its use is also a topic in its own right, and another book could be written on the tool-box and how to look after it.

In the end, we all settle for what we can afford and what we are able to use in the style of cruising that we undertake. Sometimes we look at our own lockers full of odds and ends, which have been installed with the aim of making our boat as self-sufficient as possible, even at a distance from home, then we observe that much of this gear and consumables is regularly used to get other people out of trouble.

At such moments, we should also remember all of the friends and new acquaintances who have taken time, trouble, expertise and a donation from their own spares to pop over to us when it looked as though we could do with some help.

Those are the maxims of cruising. On shore it seems to be expensive, but once your boat is well equipped and off on her travels, it becomes a very inexpensive way of living. In theory, cruising people are loners roaming the oceans exactly as they please. In practice, it is like a huge, friendly village out there, where many of us make more new, firm friends in half a year than we do in a decade ashore.

Having the spares and tools to help them out is a part of the amity.

SUMMARY

- Cruising is only good if it is free from worry.

- You can fit out your boat bit by piece – a few screws this week, a coil electric wire tomorrow.

- Safety comes first, middle and last.

- What is your survival factor? How many days could you exist without going ashore?

- Pyrotechnics: the first flare is bright and attracts attention, the second lasts long enough to pinpoint your position.

- Reserve sources of power and portable pumps are not optional extras.

- Think about it, a good dinghy makes a very usable life-raft.

- Outboard motors and folding bicycles give you your liberty and a geography away from the boat.

- The boat's tool-box must be even better than the one at home.

- Cruising is coping.

A small portable generator is useful for providing 240 volt AC mains to power tools etc. This model also has a battery charge facility.

9

ACROSS THE CHANNEL

The first trip 'across the ditch' to arrive in an overseas port is invariably spiced with excitement and adventure. With proper preparation, one hopes that it will always be tame adventure, under the crew's control. Part of this sense of adventure – even danger – is probably engendered by the popular yachting press, who rarely seem to publish the story of a cross-Channel trip during which everything went according to plan. They are following the novelist's dictum that without some form of struggle there is no story, so they hype up their copy with tales of near-misses with tankers, of being run down, of zero visibility and huge storms. Admittedly these things happen, but part of cruising fun is planning to limit the chances of a problem occurring and having already conceived a contingency plan for an immediate solution if it does.

This will be the thinking behind the scenario that follows. It is one that we hope to have planned well enough to be trouble-free, but we also hope to be able to cope if the unexpected happens. It is, in fact, a journey that we have already undertaken, but I shall enjoy replanning it with you and going over the route again, but this time with you at the helm.

This tutorial cross-Channel cruise will, in fact, be no different for having been

done before. We hope to stay lucky, but in order to give luck every encouragement, we still plan every Channel crossing as though it was the first. Our aim this time is to travel from the south coast – say our home port of Lyme Regis – across to Alderney and then on to either Guernsey or Normandy – the classic early season/ late season long weekend beer run.

The Feasibility Study

Planning actually commences quite some time before the off. We need to ensure that the tides, the weather and other circumstances make the trip feasible during the period when we want to go. We must examine four separate factors (a) the departure port (b) the planned arrival port (c) the patch of water in between (d) what we do if something goes wrong.

Planning begins by actually drawing the course line on the chart. In this instance it is a straight line, running roughly southeast and measured with the dividers as a distance of just under 70 nautical miles. From experience, we know that our boat on a long passage will maintain a speed of 4.5–6 knots, depending on tides and weather, so for simplicity's sake, we will do all our calculations and make all our

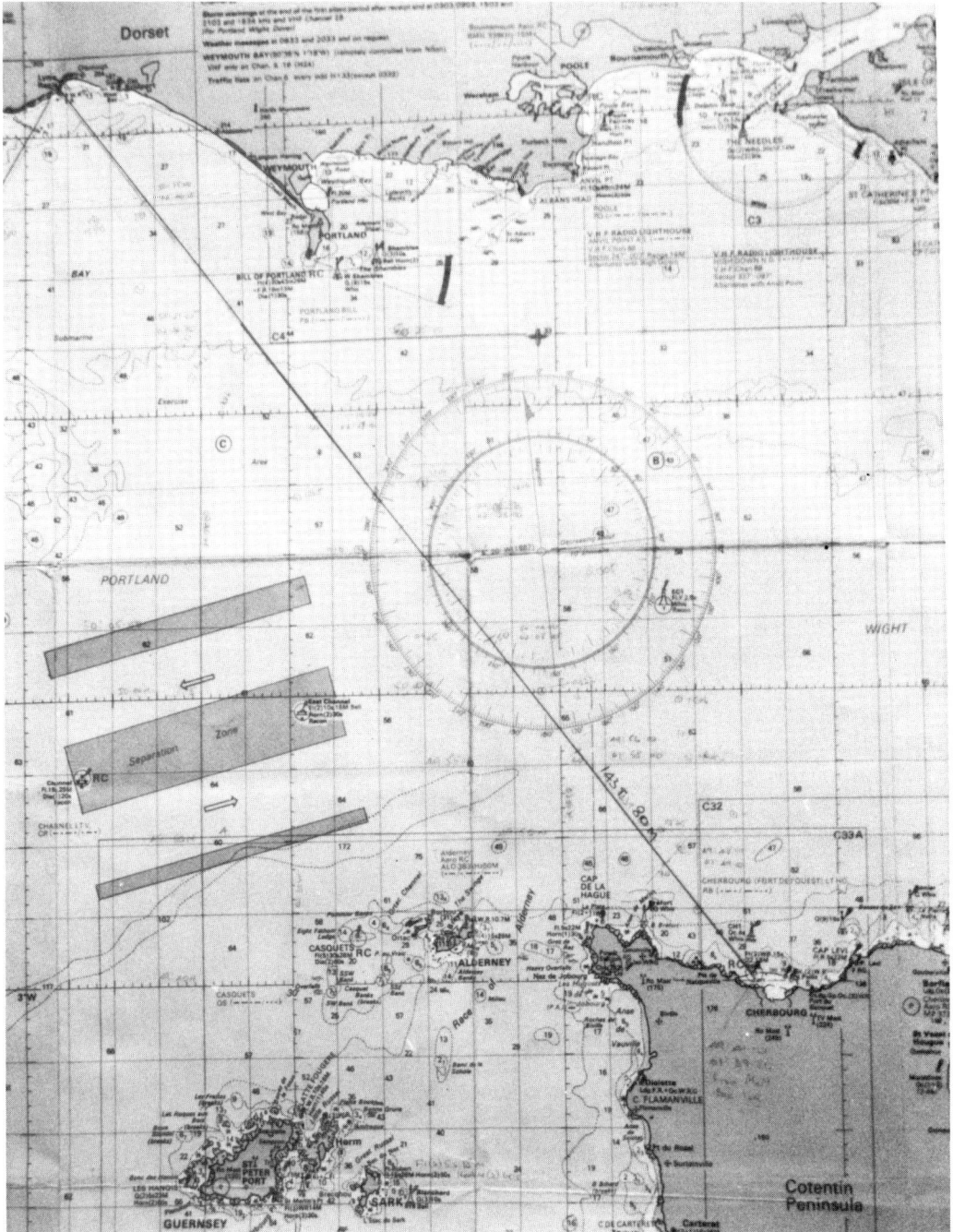

Planning begins with a straight line drawn on the chart.

assumptions on a median speed of 5 knots.

The crossing is going to take us a minimum of thirteen hours, a probable fourteen hours and possibly a bit longer. Let's go for the middle. Because we prefer to arrive in a strange port in daylight, we need to work back from our desired time of arrival in Alderney, to give the best time of departure from home. If we wish to be clever, we can extract the time of sunrise from our GPS navigator, or from an almanac, but most of us have a pretty fair idea of when it gets light and dark and that will be good enough for our purpose.

The Tide will not Wait

An informed guess reveals that on the relevant Friday, we shall have workable daylight visibility from about 0630 to 1930, varied a bit by the weather.

Our home port dries out, so we need to look at the tide tables to see when we can get off the harbour floor, to give us fourteen hours and a daylight arrival. Tidal information sources such as local tables or the almanacs published by Macmillan and Reed, give low water for the day at 0300 and a tidal range of about 2m (6.5ft). We are in Summer Time, so we work on 0400 and getting off the wall at 0530. This means that we shall have to sleep on board and will be leaving in marginal visibility.

Our home port dries out.

There are no problems about access to Alderney; you can get in at all stages of the tide, and we should be tied to a buoy before dark. If we do not make it because of weather, or some other difficulty, where are the alternative harbours? Guernsey? Just possible but a bit too far for comfort. Omonville? There is the chance of a buoy and a bit of shelter from some winds, but not a good one. Cherbourg is the obvious choice, but if we decide to divert, we shall need to make the decision quite early and will need to be careful about our course, because the tide can reach 7 knots on that corner of the Cotentin Peninsula. If we are the wrong side of the refuge port, we shall really struggle to get back up to it against the current.

The same almanacs and a couple of other pilotage books on the shelf give us plenty of information about our intended destination and our escape port. We see that Alderney is open to the north-east, probably a bit bouncy to the east and touchy with a wind from the north. This is a pity, because one of those winds would give us the best passage. The same sources show that the island's standard port for tides is St Helier and that its high-water times are roughly thirty minutes later.

The Interim

Having decided that we can go, the period up to just before the off is dominated by the lists of things to do.

1 Boat gear to pack – spares, etc.
2 Personal things like clothes and soap.
3 Food and cooking – foil, clingfilm, matches.
4 Navigation equipment – charts, almanacs, batteries.

5 A check on our finances and currency in France.
6 A list of things to do immediately before the off – HM Customs.
7 Jobs to make the house safe and secure for a week.

In this, we have assumed that your ship's log contains a list of things to do immediately you get on board. This should be a short version of the air pilot's check-off sheet, and ensures that you do not start the engine on the domestic batteries, or blow the front end of the VHF by blasting it with high voltage.

The Day Before the Off

This is a fun day, with your brain in overdrive and your nervous system just beginning to get a bit of a buzz. If you are to do it well, there is certainly no shortage of things to be done.

We are still on for 0530–1930, and the weather prospects are fair, apart from a forecast wind in the north, with a promise of south-west later. The most useful current source of mid-term forecast weather information is probably the BBC television met maps, but for the past couple of days we have listened to and watched every forecast broadcast from whatever source.

The local harbour office supplies the necessary HM Custom departure form, which is duly completed with names and passport numbers, ready to be put into the special harbourside box just before we leave. We also take the precaution of preparing a document ready for the French Customs. Even though they do not require you to fly the yellow flag Q, they are prone to come aboard, so having duplicated

Most harbours have a box for HM Customs forms.

Do the Nav Early

Because we enjoy doing it in detail, we draw in our rhumb line and work out a safe latitudinal and longitudinal arrival point close to Alderney's Braye Harbour. We also check this against the same information given in the almanacs. Next, we mark off waypoints every 10 miles (16km) along the line and also put their co-ordinates onto the provisional log sheet. These are double-checked and then keyed into the navigation black boxes, which we run at home off a 12v power supply. They should confirm that the heading and distance between these points is within a degree or so of 153 True and giving 10 miles (16km) between each. If this does not check out, we either have a duff lat/long, or somebody has hit a wrong key during the input.

That done, we turn to tides. This means reducing our local tide times to Dover, because that is the standard port for tidal flow diagrams. We are anxious about the huge tide on the corner of Normandy, so we need to know where we shall be in relation to the rhumb line when we get over the other side. We do not want to be fighting a big tide to get into Braye because we have stupidly let ourselves get too far off line at the wrong time. All cruiser skippers accept that it is inefficient to fight tide and to slow the boat down unreasonably just to hold the rhumb line. We have been as much as 15 miles (24km) off it on a cross-Channel jaunt and then been pushed back to the straight line by the contrary tide.

There is a rumour that because a sea passage from the south coast to France or the Channel Islands takes about twelve hours, this covers one complete tidal cycle, so if the tide pushed you 5 miles (8km) down Channel on the ebb, the flood

copies of all the information (in both languages) ready to hand solves a multitude of language problems.

They want to know the following: boat name, port of registry, date of registry, registration number, length, beam, draught, type of vessel (e.g. sailing cruiser), number of masts, colour of hull, colour of topsides, any visible registration numbers, owner's name, skipper's name if different, names and passport numbers of all people on board, port of departure, port of arrival in France (relevant dates for both) make and type of engine, radar, VHF, direction-finder, echo-sounder and navigation system.

A portion of this last day ashore is also reserved for more detailed navigation.

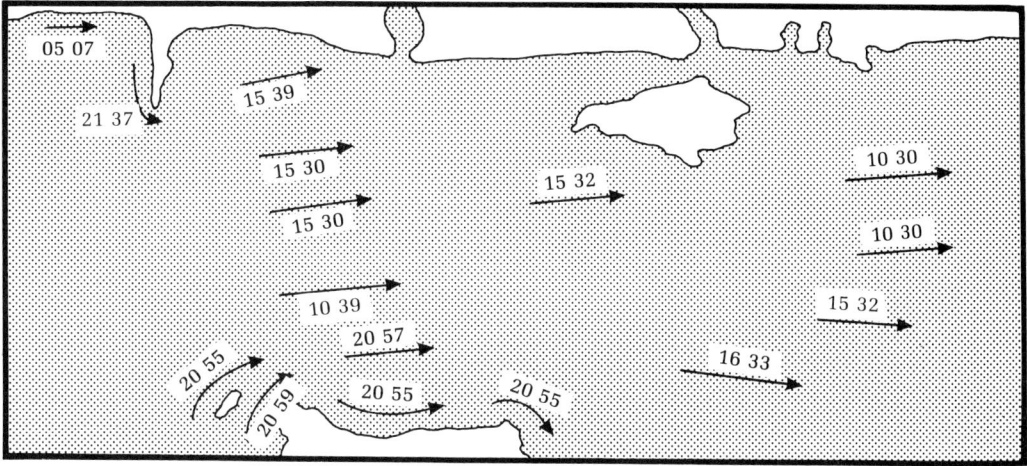

The tide is not the same on both sides of the Channel. The two-tide drift cycle is a myth.

would recover the distance. It could happen, but only rarely, as a glance at the speeds of the tide in Poole Bay and those in the Alderney Race will show. In two hours over this side, you might incur about 4 miles (6.5km) side drift at the most. Two hours off the Cap de la Hague could push you as much as 14 miles (22.5km) in either direction.

A good system for working out tidal drift on this journey is to make photocopies of the Macmillan tidal diagrams, which are written to Dover times, then to pencil in the local times, for the actual day, alongside. We try to keep ours simple. We estimate roughly where we shall be on each hour at the 5-knot average speed, and make a note that we shall be pushed 2 miles (3.2km) west between 0900 and 1000, reducing to 1.5 miles (2.4km) in the following hour, and then we shall be in slack water – and so on. By adding up the easting and westing we have an approximation of how much we shall be off the rhumb line and of roughly where we shall be if we just let the tide take us.

From this information, we deduce what action to take over the last few hours to position the boat so that she will be running approximately with the tide to get to her destination. In this instance, when we arrive within 6 miles (10km) of Alderney, the tide will be ebbing hard and pushing the boat sideways, west and down towards Guernsey, so we shall just need to make as much easting as we can when the tide is favourable earlier on. This usually involves nothing more drastic than tweaking the autopilot a couple of degrees to maximize the side shift.

The night before a cross-Channel trip is rarely one of deep, pacific sleep, so it is not a hardship to set an alarm for the 0030 weather forecast. It is still wind in the same northerly quadrant, with a suggestion of poor visibility, but we decide to go and doze in the expectancy of the 0500 alarm.

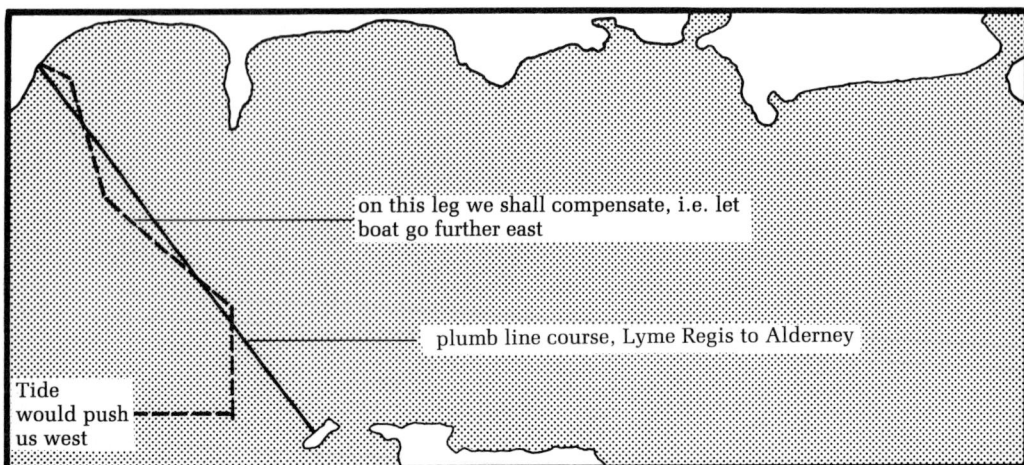

on this leg we shall compensate, i.e. let boat go further east

plumb line course, Lyme Regis to Alderney

Tide would push us west

Tide calculations show that we shall be west of Alderney, so we shall compensate somewhere along the way.

The Crossing

The buzzer rings on schedule and we can hear our keel scraping on the bottom, so we shall soon be off. All boats have their own departure routines and we settle automatically into ours. One of us makes the tea and toast, whilst the other gets off the sail covers, sees to the sea cocks and instruments and generally readies the boat for sea.

Salesmen weave all sorts of pictures of gourmet meals prepared as you sail. We have tried and failed, so we generally fall back on the alternative of several large flasks of very hot water for drinks and soup, plus a large selection of cold tempters for little and often eating.

With adequate water beneath the boat, we can still turn short round in the tiny harbour and bang on 0530 British Summer Time (BST) we are away with a light NE wind plus a touch of haze. The only real problem is a bright harbour light that dazzles your eyes and effectively kills

your night vision. Because we have done it before, we know that we can steam 090 T out through the narrow exit, then go 140 T as soon as the entrance light comes square abeam, which we see with the eyes and will also be able to observe on the radar screen. This course misses all of the mooring buoys and lobster pots in the harbour mouth. From there, our Alderney heading of 153 T also passes between the area's main rocky patches, which are always strewn with lobster pots, which are a considerable hazard in the dark. We are now very glad that we have all this information to hand, rather than be worried about the ignominy of picking up a pot before we are out of our own pond.

Clear of the harbour, we put the boat on the autopilot, set 1,500 rpm on the diesel, have a quick scan around on the radar, then both go up for'ard to set the sails. Completion of this task is rewarded by our ritualistic second cup of tea, with the boat doing her 5.5 knots at 1,100 rpm and a gentle Beaufort 2–3 on the quarter to fill

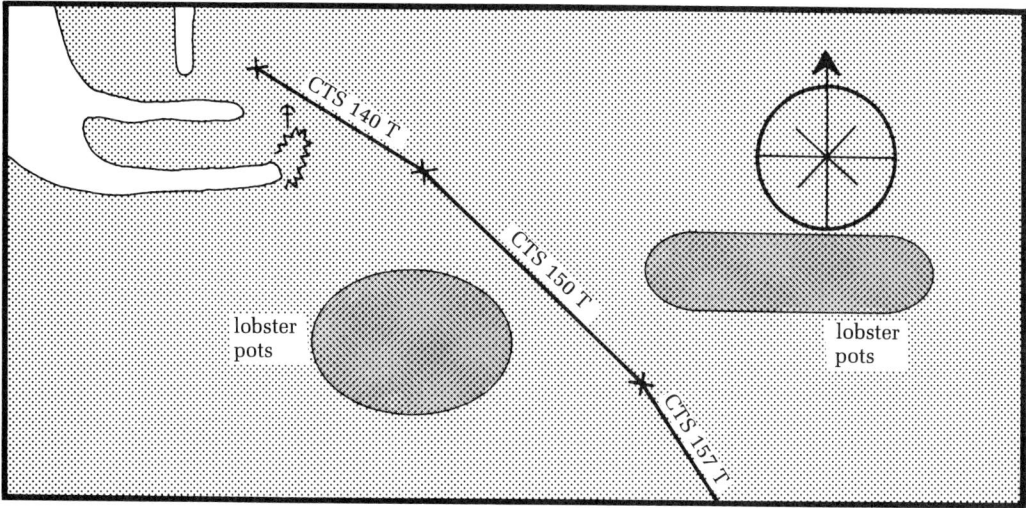

In the dark, we steer 140 to clear the harbour, then 150 to pass between the known potting areas. Then we settle on course.

all three sails, including our big genoa out on its pole. Setting this one correctly can put as much as 2 knots onto the speed.

Because we are on a long passage, we take the precaution of letting Portland coastguard know of our intentions. We are enrolled in the Small Boat Safety Scheme, and the relevant Form CG 66 is actually held by Portland, our home district. There is certain routine information that the coastguard wants to know, so this is passed to him at dictation speed, once contact has been established.

'Yacht *Abemama*, thirty, three zero, foot (9-metre) motor sailer ketch, colour green and white, CG 66 Portland leaving Lyme Regis at this time, destination Alderney, ETA (estimated time of arrival) one nine three zero local, two persons on board.'

For a jaunt of 19 miles (30km) or so along the coast, on a day when there are other boats about, we do not bother to log this information with the authorities. If we

get a problem, we can always radio it to them as it occurs. HM Coastguard has enough to do without being pestered for radio checks by boats that could call across the harbour to a friend, or having the working radio channels clogged by people just out for a picnic. On this occasion, however, we remember that it gets a bit lonely out there and we have a question mark on the visibility, so we like somebody to know where we are going. The coastguard also has the question mark and asks us if we will pass him a periodic visibility report.

From then on the trip starts to get a bit more difficult.

Cruising is Flexibility

A safe and prudent cruising crew is one that is not in a hurry and that is equipped with enough material and mental flexibility to change a plan. We have a good sea boat, but we do not go looking for rough weather to test her. We both dislike fog. If it happens, we can cope and can also stay at sea for days on end. But we prefer to keep our passage times down to reasonable levels. These capabilities are good in one respect, but in another they make you dither a bit – delay the decision to turn back.

By 0830, the visibility has closed down to 1 mile (1.6km) and by 0930 it is down to 50m (165ft). The debate is always about going on or aborting for home. After four hours of steaming we were just over 19 miles (30km) out and still about 19 miles (30km) short of the big ships using the Channel Separation Scheme lanes. Without the radar, we would heave to, or turn for home. With it, we decide to plod slowly on and hope that the fog would clear.

Radar is a fine tool, but it is also hard work to use properly. Luckily, we have picked up echoes from some trawlers in the bay and are able to fine tune the set. This gives you confidence, not so much when you can see some images on the screen, but when it is totally blank and you begin to fear that it may be off tune and down in sensitivity. The really big ships show even when the rig is not performing to maximum, but you always wonder if there might be a poor image reflector, such as a small yacht, out there and unobserved by eye or by electronics.

The morning wears uneventfully on into the afternoon and we can see the radar blips of the commercial traffic heading down towards the Channel Light Vessel, which marks the end of the controlled Separation Zone. The ships are all coming properly from left to right, just as they should do at that point. There is plenty to do and you always have a touch of pride in the way the boat and crew are doing

things. This sort of situation is not really enjoyable – but paradoxically, if you like the sea, it is not unenjoyable either.

In good visibility, crossing the shipping lanes is not only not a problem, but is also quite interesting because there is always something to see. Our interpretation of The Rules Of The Road and the Regulations For The Prevention Of Collision At Sea are quite simple here. We keep out of the way of everything over about 45 tonnes (44 tons), generally by slowing right down to let them pass ahead, just occasionally by speeding up, but most often by making a sufficient alteration of heading for our course of action to be very apparent to those on the big-ship bridge.

Today, it all goes well until we get into the 5 mile (8km) space separating the up-lane from the down. In there, you should be relatively traffic-free and able to relax a bit. But not today.

The screen shows a couple of small targets that are probably trawlers. No matter which way we headed, we cannot get rid of them, or even shift them from our bows. At one point, we even turn away far enough to get one of them directly astern, hoping to clear some distance from him, then to turn at right angles to go between both the boats that are showing. After twenty minutes, we turn, so does he, so we are back to square one.

This is a true incident, typical of the irritating part of cruising. We have taken an hour to ensure our safety, without being any closer to our destination. That too is about to alter, because the 1355 shipping forecast gives continuing north-easterly and freshening. Bye bye Alderney: hello Cherbourg – a decision which is never reached without an amount of shall we, shan't we dithering.

Having made the decision, we next

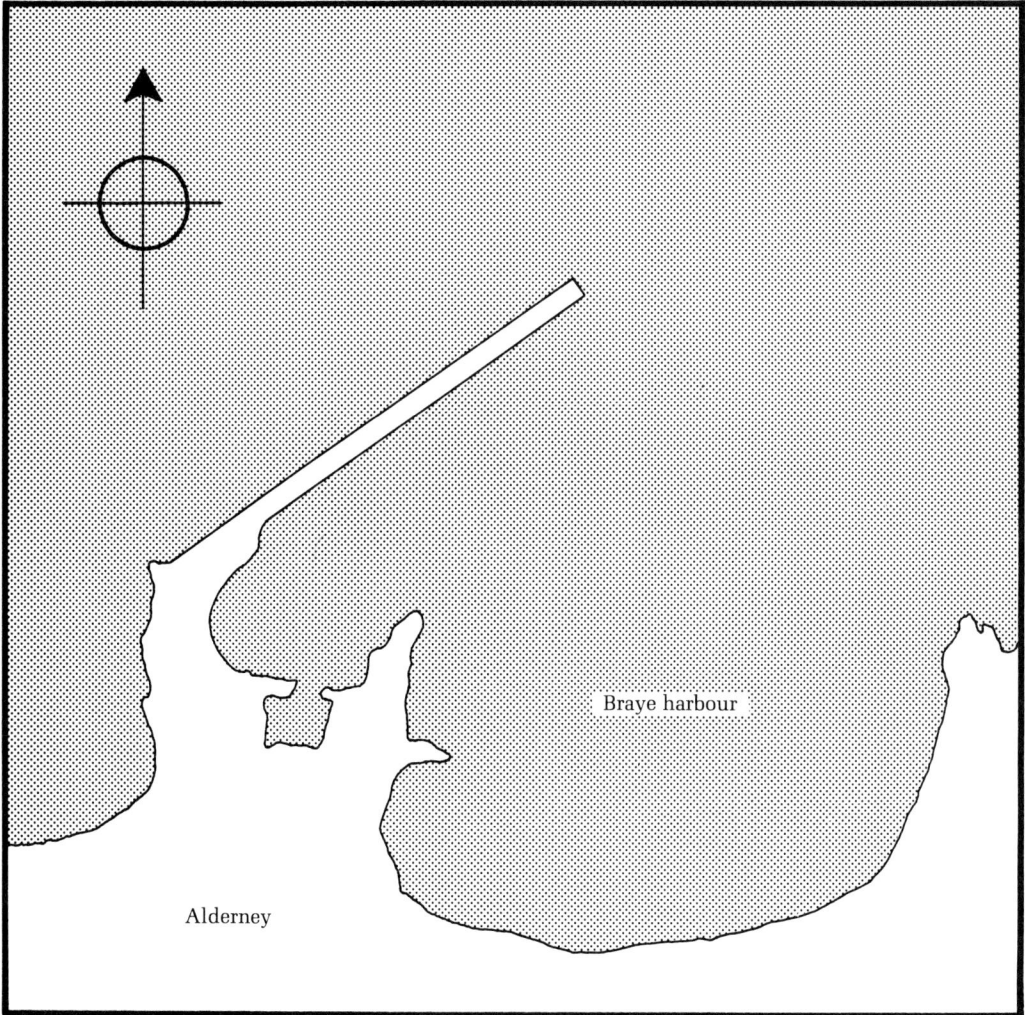

The pilot book shows that Alderney is not good in north-easterlies.

inform the coastguard of our change of intended destination and why. We could cause a real panic if we did not bother to give the new information and somebody ashore wanted to contact us urgently. At the same time, we are able to give the Portland watchkeepers a wind and visibility report, which might let them advise any other caller that it is not very pleasant out in the Big Boy Country. (It is also a nice courtesy to telephone the coastguard station to let them know that you have arrived safely. For fifty pence you keep everybody happy.)

Changing Plans

At times like this, you are very pleased

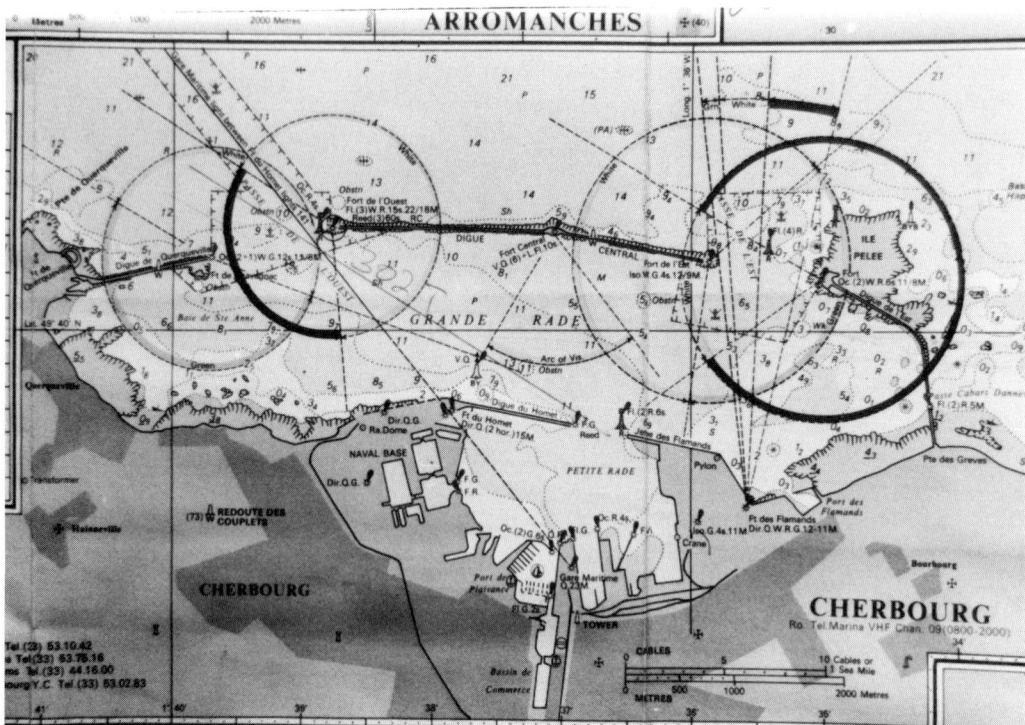

The chart of Cherbourg shows a big, wide, well-lit harbour, comparatively easy to enter even at night.

that you keep a very thorough log and have good instruments, so you know exactly where you are. At this point, out there in the fog amongst the tankers and having played position-confusing ducks and drakes with the trawlers, I am a million miles separated from the yacht club die-hards, who mock our electronics with claims that they cross the Channel with the AA map and a wetted finger. In my trad nav days, I would probably still have coped with this day's crossing, but would have been considerably less happy than I find myself when the radar, Decca, GPS and echo-sounder are all helping to tell me where I am and what everybody else within range is doing.

We are also glad that we did some work on Cherbourg before we left home and made our change of port decision early enough to assess the tide and to be able to position the boat not to fight it near the French coast. We simply give the electronic navigators the co-ordinates for Cherbourg west entrance and they come back with a course, a distance and an ETA at present speed. This is immediately checked, with a bit of arithmetic, on the chart, even though the wind is getting up and the boat is beginning to bounce – not the best time for chartwork.

Cherbourg is further than Alderney, and the predicted arrival is 2030, when it will be dark. We should, however, have a considerably lessened west-going tide, followed by slack water, at that time. Cherbourg is a big, wide harbour, well charted and well lit. We decide that we can cope, so we take the genny pole off, harden in the sheets and tell the autopilot to take us there.

Entering Harbour

From 1430 to 2030, the wind and the fog continue, then, Sod's Law being what it is, both vanish just after we have made a totally blind entrance to Cherbourg on GPS, radar, sound signals and prayers. As soon as we are inside, the long outer harbour opens up into clarity and a thousand, blinking lights. Having done the hard part in difficult conditions, we now have the easy part in good weather.

Easy? Strange harbours at night are never easy. They give even the most hardened navigators a few butterflies. Luckily, you have plenty of friends. The pilotage books give leading lights and courses to follow. The enlarged part of the chart showing the actual harbour is just about big enough to permit some form of electronic aid to position fixing. If you have been following the tides, the depth of water beneath the keel should correlate with the chart. The radar shows the harbour walls and the gaps between them and helps you to locate the buoys. Above all, you have your eyes and may even be lucky enough to see a passenger ferry or a big trawler go in. This is very useful, as long as you are certain that they are actually going to where you also want to go.

The best navigation of all, however, is to draw your own rough plan of the harbour, including the flashing characteristics of every light and mark, plus a separate list of them. Then all the crew can help to locate them and, by ticking off each as you pass, plus putting a cross on your plan, you always know exactly where you are. If you have one person to steer the boat, one to do the writing and both to watch for the lights, this is not a particularly onerous task. When you do it well, you actually get to be quite proud of yourself – a legitimate pleasure of the hobby.

The final entrance to the yacht harbour is a bit tight, and its lights are quite difficult to spot against the background until you get close. You just have to curb your impatience to be in and go slowly along the compass course that the pilot books and your chartwork have given. To waver is to die – in navigational terms, that is. The moral must be to double, even treble, check the navigational arithmetic, then to trust the instruments until your eyes can see the entrance.

Chantereyne is very well lit and the visitors' pontoon shown in the pilot book is very clearly marked. We put the boat onto an end pontoon and stroll down to find a better berth. There is no problem and, with now zero wind, berthing will not be difficult. By 2130 we have telephoned news of our arrival back to home and are enjoying a shower and a drink, accompanied by the smell of pre-cooked frozen lasagne coming alive in the oven.

It has been a long day, made longer by our change of destination. Now that the weather conditions have bettered, we could have been enjoying Alderney after all. But Cherbourg is a good place to be, and cruising is fun wherever you are.

By midnight, any doubts that we might have had about the wisdom of our change of plan are totally dissipated by a rising north-east wind, which persists for three days. We stay snug on our berth until Tuesday, when we saunter out to help some wet, exhausted crews who have been gale-pinned and banging about in an Alderney made too difficult to evacuate because of rough, wind-over-tide conditions in the notorious Race.

Cruising is coping and having well-laid flexible plans, plus a boat as well equipped as your finances will allow, with which to complete the enjoyment.

So, you sit in places like Cherbourg and listen to the wind, and when you have proved yourself to be invincible at Scrabble, you get out the maps and charts and pilotage books and – even before you have shaken off the effects of an elongated, rough day at the start of this voyage – you begin to get a bit of a yen to start planning a long cruise down to the Canary Isles – at least.

SUMMARY

- The first foreign port is a landfall you will never forget.

- The importance of a feasibility study.

- Be prepared to spend a long time verifying tidal information on harbours and *en route* – they will be a major planning factor.

- Cruise planning is lists, check-lists and even more lists. When you are out at sea there is no corner shop to make up the shortfall.

- Do you know the customs regulation? Out? Home?

- Charts, almanacs, pilotage books, logbooks – expensive but essential.

- Make your first crossing in daylight.

- Have a written flexible alternative plan.

- Swallow your pride. If there is a pilot, follow him – but only if you are completely sure that he is going safely where you want to go.

- When in doubt, forget your hunches: believe the instruments.

GLOSSARY

Abaft   Behind.

Abeam   At the side of the centre section of the boat.

Adrift   A boat or item that is loose or un-moored.

Aft   The back of the boat.

Ahead   In the front part of the boat.

Amidships   In the centre of the boat.

Astern   Behind the boat, reverse etc.

Athwartships   Across the boat.

Awash   At the same level as the water.

Ballast   Weight placed in the lower part of a boat to give stability and trim.

Bar   A shallow spit of sand/mud across a harbour entrance.

Beam   Width of the boat, usually measured from a central position.

Bear off   Move off from a quayside mooring.

Belay   Securing a warp or rope around a cleat, bollard etc.

Below   Inside the cabin of the boat.

Bight   A loop in the centre section of a rope.

Bilge   The very bottom of the inside of a boat.

Bitter end   The last link in the anchor chain.

Boat hook   A pole or staff with a hook at one end.

Bollard   Stout mooring post.

Bow   The front of a boat.

Broach   The boat swings quickly side on to the oncoming waves.

Bulkhead   An internal partition separating cabins etc.

Bulwarks   A low, solid railing around the deck area.

Buoy   A floating navigation mark.

Casting off   Letting go a mooring rope.

Cleat   A special deck fitting to which ropes can be tied off and secured.

Coaming   The raised section surrounding the cockpit.

Cockpit   The area (usually at the stern) for the crew to sit in to control the boat.

Deck   The walkable surface above decks.

Dinghy   A small open craft used on larger boats as a tender.

Displacement   The total weight of the boat.

Draft   The amount of the boat that sits below the waterline.

Fairlead   A special fitting at deck level into which the mooring ropes are guided.

Fairway   The unencumbered, navigable channel.

Fathom   A unit of measurement for six feet.

Fender   Plastic air-filled bags used to protect the sides of a vessel.

Fiddle rail   Bolt-on attachment to the cooker to stop pans from sliding off the rings.

Flake   To lay the anchor rope or chain in a loose figure eight on deck.

Flukes   The pointed parts of an anchor.

Freeboard   The amount of measurable deck above the waterline.

Galley   The cooking area aboard a boat.

Gimbals   A swinging pivot which keeps the cooker/compass *et al* upright at all times.

Ground tackle   The anchor and its associated warps and chain.

Gunwale   The joint between the topsides and the deck.

Heads   The name for the boat's toilet facility.

Helm   The steering position.

Helmsman   The person doing the steering at tiller or wheel.

Holding ground   The type of seabed (mud, shale, rock, etc.) used when anchoring.

Inboard   The area inside or on the boat.

GLOSSARY

Jury rig A rudder or mast etc. made from other parts of the boat in an emergency.

Keel The spine of the boat or the weighted section under the hull.
Knot The unit of speed for one nautical mile per hour.

Lee side The side of the boat opposite to the wind.
Leeward Away from the direction of the wind.
Leeway The drift of the boat sideways caused by the action of the wind.
Lifejacket A safety device that is supposed to keep a person afloat.
Log An electrical or mechanical device to measure the boats speed and distance through the water.
Logbook A record kept aboard of navigational details of a voyage.

Make fast Securing a warp to a cleat or bollard.
Mooring Tying up alongside or to a swinging buoy.

Nautical mile A unit of measurement equal to approximately 2,000 yards.

Outboard Outside the boat; portable petrol-driven propulsion unit.
Overfalls A confused area of water where two tidal systems meet.

Painter A mooring rope for a small dinghy or tender.
Port The left-hand side of a boat looking forward.
Pulpit The guard-rail that surrounds the bow area.
Pushpit The guard-rail that surrounds the stern area.

Quarter A rear corner of a boat.

Riding light The white anchor light.
Rowlock A swivel bracket on the gunwale of a rowing boat to hold the oar.
Rubbing strake Timber, plastic or rubber fendering in a strip to protect the sides of a boat.
Rudder A flat blade which swivels underwater at the stern used for steering the boat.

Scuppers Drain holes low down in the bulwarks.
Seizing A lashing joint that holds two warps together.
Set of tide The direction in which the tide runs.
Shackle A metal fitting with a screw gate.
Shank The long arm of an anchor.
Sheer To swing the anchor about.
Shoal water Very shallow, fast running water.
Slack water The period at which there is no measurable tidal flow.
Sounding The depth of water shown on the chart.
Spring An extra one or two mooring lines that prevent fore and aft movement on a quayside.
Stanchion A stout post supporting the sea railing.
Starboard The right-hand side of the boat looking forward.
Steerage way Sufficient speed to allow the rudder to alter the boat's course.
Stem The front of the bow.
Stern The back part of the boat.

Tender A small boat carried aboard and used for getting ashore.
Thwart A small wooden or plastic seat in the tender or dinghy.
Tiller The long shaft of wood or metal connected to the rudder and used for steering.
Topsides The section of the boat above the waterline.
Transducer A device used to relay and emit echo signals for soundings.

Underway The boat, when moving through the water unattached.
Up and down When the anchor warp is in a vertical attitude.

Wake The trail of foam, wavelets left astern of a moving boat.
Warp A term for a rope or line.
Watch A section of time that a person spends steering, navigating etc.
Wind rode The boat lying to wind when at anchor.

Yaw To wander either side of a predetermined course.

INDEX

Alderney, 119–20
anchors and anchoring,
 41–59
 anchor capstan, 27
 anchor station, keeping, 27
 anchor watch, 26
 bearings, 52
 bedding in, 51
 bitter end, 59
 bower anchor, 56
 calculating scope, 53
 catenation effect, 43–4
 choosing, 41
 effect of wind/tide on, 42
 electric winches, 50
 flaking for ease, 49
 flukes, 42
 fouling of, 44
 holding-off, 86
 holding ground, 41, 45
 kedge, 42, 55–6
 letting go, 49
 line of pull, 44
 log, 52
 marking chain, 50
 picnic, 42
 risk of fouling moorings,
  48
 second anchor, 56
 setting of, 44
 settling two, 57
 sounder, use of in, 46
 stowage of, 41
 trip line, 53
 types of, 41–2
 'up and down', 50
 warp, 43
 weight table, 43
ascendeur, 106–7
Auxiliary Coastguards, 93

backed jib, 37

basic seamanship, 29
battery charger, 99
berthing, 60–81
 against craft, 66, 69–70
 classic assists, 65
 in a marina, 75
 in a tide, 66
 in a wind, 65
 on the swing, 77
 short handed brake, 67
 using springs, 67
 using the prop, 11
 using warps, 66
bilge keels, 71
 drying out on, 71
boarding ladder, 19
boat bikes, 105
boat handling, 33
boat hook and warp, 78
boom, 38
bow thruster, 16
bowline, 29
Bruce anchor, 41
buoyancy aids, 97
burgees, 91

Cardinal buoyage, 30
Channel crossing, 112–24
Cherbourg, 122–4
circuit tester, 109
cold weld compounds, 107
coming alongside, 65
common terms, 28
contra-rotating props, 15
cordage locker, 88–9
cost of cruising, 25
CQR anchor, 41
crew, 23
crossing the Channel,
 112–24
 changing plans, 121–23
 checklist, 115

entering harbour, 123–4
HM Customs box, 116
navigation, 116–17
planning, 112
tides, 114–15
cruiser-racers, 34
cruising log, 94

Danforth anchor, 41
diesel engines, 9
dinghy, 102–5
down-pull cords, 38
Dragon-type racer, 34
dressing the ship, 92
drying out, 71

efficiency chest, 109
electrical tester, 109
emergency repairs, 106
engine spares, 108–9
English Channel, 112–24
equipment, 96–111
 transport of, 105

family cruiser layout, 25
fenders, 77
'ferry glide' mode, 62
fin keelers, 16, 72–3
fitting out the boat, 96–111
flags, 91–2
 correct use, 92
 regulations, 92
flare pack, 98
flares, use of, 98–9
folding bikes, 105
forestay, 39–40
Fortress anchor, 42
fuses, 107

G clamps, 107
generator, 109
genoa sail, 39

INDEX

going to sea, 33–40
going upwind, 33, 37
grease pressure, 15
grease reservoir, 14
gybing, 37

hacksaw to clear prop, 19
Halberg Rassy, 23
halyard frapping, 79
heaving to, 37
heavy-weather jacket, 98
hitches, 29
how the boat works, 28–32

IALA buoyage system, 30
ideal boat crew, 26
in-mast furling, 38
insulating tape, 108

jiffy reefing, 38

lateral drift, 22
Law of Motion, 16
laying, 58
leeway, 22
life-jackets, 97
life-rafts, 102–5
liquid insulation, 108
Log, 94
lying athwart, 38

mains lead, 109
marina manners, 79
marina reversing, 76
masthead-rigged genoa, 40
Meon anchor, 41
mizzen sail, 39
mole grips, 107
mooring in strong winds,
    26–7
motive power, 8
motor sailers, 9

navigation, 29
navigation lights, 30–2
negative wind pressure, 22

outboard motor, 105

part-time cruiser, 34

picking up a buoy, 61–4
    diagonal approach, 64
    under sail, 64
piggy-back spring, 84
pilot mark spotting, 29
pipe repair kit, 108
portable generators, 109
portable power pack, 100
propeller, 12
    balance, 11
    calculating diameter of, 12
    cleaning, 18
    diameter, 11
    effect, 9
    maintenance, 16
    mechanical cutters, 18
    pitch, 12
    rope around, 18
    using to move off, 19
    walking, 9
pumps, 100
    electric, 100
    hand, 100

Q flag, 91

radar, 120
Red Ensign, 92
reduction gearbox, 13
reefing, 38
reefing points, 38
roller reefing headsails, 39
ropes, 88–9
rope snubber, 58
rucksacks, 105
rudder action/reaction, 17
rudder effects, 16
Rules of the Road, 30, 94

safety aids, whereabouts of,
    29
safety equipment, 97
safety harnesses, 98
sail hanks, 40
sailing close hauled, 37
screws, 107
shaft brake, 14
shaft grease gland, 14
shaft lubrication, 14
shearing about, 89

Ship's Log, 94
shore transits, 27
short turn, 76
signal mirror, 98
signalling pack, 98
single bladed props, 13
single sail handling, 40
single screw cruiser, 9
single screw turning, 15
slab reefing, 38
slimline for speed, 34
snorkel mask, 102
sound signals, 92–4
    chart of, 93
Spain, 23
spotlight, 99
springer lines, 20
stern spring, 83
stuffing box, 14
stuffing gland, 14
suction gripper, 102

taking the ground, 70
timber, 102
tools, 108
torch, 98
towing, 89
    alongside, 90
    knots, 91
trawler type hull, 34
Treguier, 82–3
    manoeuvre, 84
turning with the prop, 11
twin power units, 9
twin screw cruiser, 15

unberthing, 82–7
    holding-off anchor, 86
    reversing out, 85
    using looped warp, 84
    warping across, 85

variable pitch, 13
VHF radio, 75

watchkeeping, 23–4
weather helm, 37
whistle, 98
White Ensign, 92
wood plugs, 102